Philip

D1486529

Oxfordshire and Buckinghamshire Pubs

Oxfordshire and Buckinghamshire Pubs

John Camp

drawings by Brian O. Hall

B. T. BATSFORD LTD
LONDON

First published 1965

Printed and bound in Great Britain
by Jarrold and Sons Ltd, London and Norwich
for the publishers B. T. Batsford Ltd
4 Fitzhardinge Street, Portman Square, London W1

This book is dedicated to my wife, who bore, stoically, my many absences from the fold in search of material, and never once made a joke about barmaids

Acknowledgment

*My thanks are due to the many landlords who took so
much trouble to supply the information I required.
I am also indebted to certain undergraduates of the University
of Oxford, whose intimate knowledge of the City
taverns could never have been acquired without a Government Grant.*

Author's note

OXFORDSHIRE AND BUCKINGHAMSHIRE are well provided with village inns and pubs. There are about 1800 of them in the two counties, and this book describes a representative cross-section. Though Tudor buildings abound (half-timbered in Buckinghamshire and Cotswold stone in Oxfordshire) the pubs dealt with range from ancient inns, like The Ostrich at Colnbrook, to the modern design and architecture of the new housing estates and pubs found at Witney and Bletchley.

Many are village inns, but others are main-road hostelries carrying on the old tradition of the coaching-inns of former days. But each has its own particular character and atmosphere, and it is this I have tried to capture in the pages that follow.

The 'atmosphere' of a pub is a most elusive thing to define. The 'regular' will find it difficult to say just what it is that attracts him in his own 'local'. Faced with the question he will almost certainly reply that he likes 'the company'. This may well be so, but it tells us little about the pub itself. One may spend a riotous evening with friends in a pub with about as much charm as Pentonville Prison. But the most attractive décor and picturesque ingle-nooks will mean nothing if the place is deserted and the landlord morose. And this, of course, is the answer. Whether the decoration is ancient woodwork or plain plaster, the atmosphere is created by the landlord. Unobtrusively and imperceptibly he sets the tone, drawing the stranger into the conversation if he thinks it wise, or merely acknowledging his presence and custom with a few remarks about the weather. At the same time he must continually walk the slippery tight-rope between saloon and public-bar, giving equal attention to both sides and giving neither cause for complaint.

It therefore follows that my impression of the atmosphere found in the pubs dealt with in this book have been formed largely by the attitude of the landlord and his staff.

To do justice to even half the pubs in the two counties would be impossible in a book of this size. I have concentrated mainly on those which are still genuine pubs, rather than hotels or licensed restaurants, which many pubs are becoming today. I have also included many village inns off the beaten track, leaving out the better-known ones which have been written about elsewhere. It is to be hoped that, even if your favourite pub is not mentioned this time, you will be compensated by the fact that others are included which may be new to you, and you will be encouraged to explore further.

Finally, a word about the licensing-hours. Basically these are 10 am to 2.30 pm, and 6 pm to 10.30 pm weekdays. In Buckinghamshire there is an extension to 11 pm on Fridays and Saturdays, but in Oxfordshire this applies on Saturdays only. No doubt in order to avoid any sense of conformity, the Wexham area of Slough has no extension on Fridays *or* Saturdays, closing at 10.30 pm as for the rest of the week. Sundays hours are 12 noon to 2 pm, and 7 pm to 10.30 pm. Happily this applies to both counties.

One day, perhaps, opening-hours will be standard all over the country. For the time being the existing system prevails, confusing the British and bewildering the foreign tourist. But there is plenty to see in Oxfordshire and in Buckinghamshire even outside licensed hours, and some indication of this has been made in this book. Cheers!

Amersham, 1965   J.C.

I
Oxfordshire

ASTON ROWANT

The Lambert Arms

Free House. Bedrooms 13 Hotel, 7 Motel. *Food* Restaurant. *Special drinks* Courage's E.I.P.A. *Route* A40 London–Oxford. *Nearest station* Princes Risborough. *Telephone* Kingston Blount 496.

This old coaching-inn is situated on the A40 London–Oxford road at the foot of the Chilterns, and at the junction with the Watlington to Chinnor road. In such a position it is not surprising that it was famous during the coaching era, and was one of the best-known inns on this busy road.

Externally it still has the look of an old building, and the bar and rooms adjoining are very much what they have always been. There are the usual massive beams, stone floors, and comfortable, mellow, atmosphere of the more substantial old-world hostelry. But there is also something more. The A40 is busier these days than it has ever been. Gone are the stage-coaches, but the travellers on the road have increased mightily since the days of Dickens. The Lambert Arms has adapted itself to cater for these, and in addition to the old building there is now a motel with every requirement the modern traveller may need. Wisely, the charm of the old building has been left, and the motel is a separate entity with its own character. The two buildings, one old and one new, sit happily side-by-side, a pleasant and harmonious blend of two very different architectural styles.

There is a lovely garden, with views of Aston Woods and Beacon Hill, and although the site is at an important cross-roads it is a surprisingly peaceful place with few buildings near by.

The Lambert Arms is a free house, and easy to find, despite the seeming confusion and complexity of the various localities mentioned on the brochure.

The postal address is Aston Rowant, the telephone exchange is Kingston Blount, and the telegraphic address Lewknor. Although the county boundary is not much more than a mile away at least it is in Oxfordshire, and The Lambert Arms has been spared the fate of near-by Stokenchurch, originally Oxfordshire, but transferred to Buckinghamshire in 1895. This would have been too much!

BAMPTON

The Talbot Inn

Brewer Ind Coope. *Bedrooms* 6. *Food* 'Bistro' Restaurant, Snacks. *Route* A4095 Faringdon–Witney. *Nearest station* Witney. *Telephone* Bampton Castle 326.

Opinions on Bampton seem widely divergent. One guide to Oxfordshire describes it as 'noteworthy', whilst another writer calls it 'most obscure'. It is quiet and seemingly remote, set in the flat meadowland west of Oxford, on the Faringdon to Witney road.

The Talbot takes its name from the Earls of Leicester, who occupied the castle until 1700. But even then the inn was old, and a hostelry is reputed to have been on the site as far back as the thirteenth century. It stands facing the main square, neat and trim, with little to indicate its great age or the secrets within. For here a ghost is said to prowl, bumping in the corridors at night and waking the residents with heavy footsteps in the early morning. But ghosts are common in Bampton. A house near the church was plagued for many years, and at the cross-roads, where suicides were buried, spectral figures are said to have been seen.

None of this worries The Talbot. The two little bars continue to give cheer to the traveller and local alike, and form a perfect view-point for the Morris Dancing for which the village is famous, and which takes place every Whit-Monday on the square.

Ind Coope are responsible for the beer, the licensee for the excellent snacks available. Presumably he is also responsible for naming the public-bar *Le Bistro*—an odd continental touch to find in this most English of villages.

BANBURY

The Crown

Brewer Hunt Edmunds. *Food* Restaurant. *Route* A423. *Nearest station* Banbury. *Telephone* Banbury 3797.

The traveller from London to Birmingham or Stratford-on-Avon will almost certainly go through Banbury. It is less certain if he will appreciate the charm of this famous town or see much of its many ancient buildings unless he stops and explores. For the main part of the town is away from the main road and is reached by turning right at the Cross. Down this way, tucked in the corner of Bridge Street, is The Crown, a handsome building now part of the Hunt Edmunds group. It has been largely rebuilt, and perhaps one might wish that the front elevation had been given the same treatment as the delightful modern interior. As it is, and perhaps as a sop to local opinion, the architects have reverted to 'Brewers' Tudor' and played for safety. But inside it is very different. No fake beams or Birmingham-made brassware here. The lounge-bar is a beautifully proportioned room, light and elegant, with modern furniture which is attractive and comfortable. A splendid fireplace of clean Cotswold stone dominates the room and blends happily with the light woodwork and modern floor-coverings.

Round the walls is an amazing collection of photographs and maps—the only reminder of the past in the place. For these are railway photographs, mainly G.W.R., tracing the history and development of that most individual of lines. Here we may see Bradshaw's first maps of 1842, trace the transition from broad- to narrow-gauge, and examine at leisure the many dramatic photographs of steam at work. It is a fascinating collection—all the more fascinating to find in such a setting.

Apart from the fact that The Crown is near the station, it has no particular connection with railways. A Hunt Edmunds director is a railway enthusiast. He is to be complimented on using his hobby to such advantage, and entertaining his customers in this pleasant way.

BANBURY

The Inn Within

Free House. Food Winston Restaurant. *Special drinks* Mitchell & Butler's Brew Eleven, Worthington E, Whitbread, Double Diamond. *Route* A423. *Nearest station* Banbury. *Telephone* Banbury 2920.

The good people of Banbury seem to have spent the last three hundred years destroying anything of value the town possessed. Banbury Cross, of nursery-rhyme fame, has not existed since the Commonwealth and the edifice at the cross-roads which marks the original site was put up in 1859, in an age not noted for its good taste.

From the direction of Stratford The Inn Within is just across the road to the left of the 'cross'. It is a pub of many parts and many surprises.

It is a free house, but might better be described as 'free-for-all' house. Victorian in design, one of the several barn-like bars is decorated almost entirely with mirrors, the result being an impression of being in the centre of a long series of identical rooms stretching away into the void. Although this is the feature which has given the pub its name, it seems hardly necessary to have created it as there really are an enormous number of rooms in this vast edifice. Not that they are all bars, of course. Included in the building is the Winston Restaurant, a Winter Garden and a dance-hall. But it doesn't stop there. At various times one may enjoy roller-skating, all-in wrestling, or simply relax and watch a boxing-match! The pub has been in the same family for over a hundred years, and present lady licensee claims to be the only woman boxing-promoter in Great Britain.

The Inn Within is quite a place—and needless to say beloved by the coach-parties which always seem to be roaming round the town at any hour of the day or night. Possibly a knowledge of all-in wrestling is an asset when dealing with some of the more restive customers—but to run the place at all the good lady certainly has to have her skates on!

BANBURY

The Reindeer   PARSONS STREET

Brewer Hook Norton Brewery. *Food* Snacks at bar. *Route* A41. *Nearest Station* Banbury. *Telephone* Banbury 29221.

In these days of mammoth take-overs the complicated ramifications of the brewing industry are often taken for granted. But independent breweries still exist, and the Hook Norton Brewery Company, which owns The Reindeer, is one of them. The Reindeer, in one of the oldest streets in the town, claims to be the oldest inn. Certainly the date 1570 carved on the massive door of the old archway is a pointer, though much of the original structure is a hundred years older than this. Outside, The Reindeer advertises itself by way of an eye-catching sign extending almost across the street, for in this narrow thoroughfare one is so close to the buildings that it is very easy not to notice them.

Internally The Reindeer is a warren of passages and small rooms, with only one bar. There is a smoke-room, but the pub centres on the public-bar where darts and dominoes are played with great intensity and, on occasions, to the great discomfort of the drinker.

The great glory of The Reindeer was, at one time, the Globe Room. The room is still there, reached by a short flight of stone steps from the yard outside, but the glory has gone. This was the magnificent plaster ceiling and panelling said to have been designed by Inigo Jones. Ceiling and panelling were removed and sold to an American collector, but before this act of desecration could be completed an enlightened corporation bought them back, and happily they remain in this country. Unhappily they were not re-installed in the Globe Room, but now await their final resting-place as part of the new Civic Centre. The Globe Room is still an attractive room, even though shorn of its former beauty. There is still plenty of panelling in other parts of this inn which the corporation might like. On the whole, though, it might be a simpler solution, and cause less upheaval, if The Reindeer were to be used as the Civic Centre. At least the ceiling and panelling would be back in their right setting.

BANBURY

The Unicorn   MARKET PLACE

Brewer Hunt Edmunds. *Food* Snacks. *Route* A41. *Nearest station* Banbury. *Telephone* Banbury 3396.

Fronting on to the Market Place, The Unicorn exhibits a mixture of styles separated by five hundred years. At the side of the archway, with its great gates, modern shop-fronts have replaced the original exterior. Above them the three gables of the old building and the massive chimneys still look down on the busy scene, the timbers warped and twisted, the plaster ancient and crumbling.

Through the arch, and we are back in the past. But not as far back as might be thought. Stone statues and an impressive wrought-iron staircase take us back to Victorian times rather than to Elizabethan, though one may still find part of the old galleries so typical of coaching-inns, and the stairs leading from the cobbled yard.

The small saloon-bar of The Unicorn is unpretentious and uninspiring. The public-bar, however, is a very different story. Here again is the impression of being in the presence of a mid-Victorian restoration scheme, now as dated, but to many as interesting, as the earlier building must have been. The effect is heightened by the quite extraordinary collection of helmets, weapons, uniforms and martial bric-à-brac suspended from the ceiling and decorating the walls. Pikes and helmets from the Civil War are there, swords and pistols abound. On the counter the handsome model of a woman catches the eye and seems vaguely familiar. But this is no Greek goddess holding a leaflet in her hand. She is, in fact, in retirement after a great many years advertising a famous tea, and she and her sisters were once familiar sights in grocers' windows up and down the country.

Like The Crown, in Bridge Street, this is a Hunt Edmunds inn. But here the similarity ends. Except, perhaps, that in both pubs there is so much to see that there is a danger of 'Time' being called long before one's quota has been reached.

BENSON-ON-THAMES

The Chicken in the Basket

Free House. Food Restaurant. *Special drinks* Whitbread's Tankard. *Route* A423 Wallingford–Oxford. *Nearest station* Wallingford. *Telephone* Benson 331.

If this place is a pub at all, it is certainly one of the most sophisticated for a long way. Strictly speaking it is a licensed restaurant of a high standard where one may dine and dance in extraordinary comfort.

It stands right on the Oxford to Henley road, at the junction to the little village of Benson and the road to Ewelme and Watlington. It is modern and very attractive externally, exhibiting some surprisingly effective ideas in design. Although a long way removed from the village inn or city tavern

16

it is still a pub, in that there is a bar for the casual caller who prefers to drink rather than to dine and dance.

The most interesting thing about this place is that the bar is on the roof! Furthermore it is designed in Swedish style, flat-topped with no outside walls but a balcony running along two sides of the room.

Despite the smoothness of the dining-and-dancing clientèle downstairs, the customers are typical of bars anywhere. Local villagers, farmers, the young and the old are all in evidence, the only requirement being the ability to scale a long flight of stairs.

As with many restaurants this is a free licence, and the beer is all pressurised. No wood casks here, though the Mackeson's and Tankard Keg provided serve as an admirable substitute. Indeed, at least one rustic has felt sufficiently cheered to descend to the dance-floor below with the intention of polishing-up his polka, though this is not encouraged by the management. Still, The Chicken in the Basket is something different, even if it is unlikely to be the pub of the future.

The Chicken in the Basket

BICESTER

The Six Bells

Brewer Phipps. *Food* Snacks. *Route* A41. *Nearest station* Bicester. *Telephone* Bicester 578

The date 1682 on the wall of this pub in King's End is misleading. No doubt it refers to the present building but in fact there has been an inn on the site since 1472, the oldest licence in the town. These days it belongs to Phipps, the Northampton brewers, and is a very cheery and pleasant pub. The tiny saloon-bar, with its counter only about three feet long, is hardly the place to accommodate a coach party, though this could easily be done in the public. Despite its age The Six Bells does not make a particular feature of this asset, believing that there are enough old pubs around the country which tend to live in the past and forget the present-day requirements of their customers.

As a result it is bright and brisk, the only concession to old age being some once-used agricultural instruments on the walls and a display of Victorian ornaments of limited attraction.

Apart from this The Six Bells is concerned with being a pub, and this it does with the utmost efficiency. The name implies that it is near the church, though this now has a ring of eight bells. The Six Bells believes in keeping up-to-date, but is unlikely to change its name on this score.

BICESTER

The White Lion

Brewer Courage. *Food* Snacks. *Special drinks* Draught Cider. *Route* A41. *Nearest station* Bicester. *Telephone* Bicester 4088.

This pleasant little market-town stands on the road from London to Birmingham, the A41. The town has little history to record and is peaceful enough, though it has the tang of hunting with its many saddlers and harness-makers' shops squeezed in between the garish shop-fronts of the multiple grocers.

The White Lion is the oldest inn in Bicester, though others may boast older licenses. The building is ancient, really ancient, and little has been done in the way of modernisation.

The low front door leads into a dark passage, with a rather neglected lounge on the left and the old yard straight ahead. On the right there is another much larger room with an unusual atmosphere. This is due to the fact that it is a very long room and slopes down to the bar at the far end. In addition the ceiling beams are so low that anyone of even normal height must bend his head and make the journey to the bar as though deep in prayer.

Many of the beams are covered with beer-mats of every kind, both English and foreign, and on the wall is an entertaining broad-sheet explaining that the reason men live longer than most animals is because no animals drink alcohol.

Courage are the brewers here, and there is very good draught cider.

BIX

The Fox

Brewer Henley Brewery Co. *Food* Snacks. Coffee until noon. *Special drinks* Whitbread's Tankard. *Route* A423 Henley–Wallingford. *Nearest station* Henley-on-Thames. *Telephone* Henley 134.

Out of Henley a fine, wide road runs north to Nettlebed and Oxford. The beginning of this is the famous Henley 'Fair Mile' and three miles further The Fox stands by the roadside in seeming isolation, though the little hamlets of Bix and Bix Bottom are not far away.

It is a large pub dating from the 1930s, and built with an eye to the passing trade along this busy road. There is a massive car-park, a large garden, and, one would think, plenty of room inside. Surprisingly enough the bars are not very big, and on summer evenings, with the car-park full, the garden really comes into its own.

The owners are the Henley Brewery Company, and as well as their own beers Whitbread's Tankard is available from the keg. Needless to say, food and snacks are available at all times and coffee is served mornings until noon.

The saloon-bar has a slightly Victorian air about it, created by the rather heavy panelling but due, largely, to an immense and intricately carved mirror dating from 1860.

Considering the size of the pub in relation to the size of the bars there must be an enormous number of rooms behind the scenes. This is confirmed by the licensee, who has the onerous task of supervising the locking of over fifty doors on the premises before retiring at night. The legend on the wall describing the 'perfect landlord' is a variation of the one usually met with, but even this does not list this particular attribute.

BURFORD

The Lamb   SHEEP STREET

Free House. Bedrooms 12. *Food* Restaurant. *Special drinks* Worthington E, Flowers' I.P.A., Garnes Special. *Route* A40 London–Gloucester. *Nearest station* Shipton-under-Wychwood. *Telephone* Burford 3155.

Of the many lovely Cotswold villages, Burford, to many people, is the loveliest. The steep high street runs down from the main London–Gloucester road to the narrow banks of the Windrush, that most delightfully named of all rivers. Stone is everywhere in the Cotswolds, from the open country with fields bounded by dry-stone walls to the villages and towns where every house and building is of the same material. And yet there is no monotony.

The Lamb is a perfect example of Tudor stone construction. Long and low, it stands at the junction of two streets and seems even more solid as a result than the adjacent buildings.

The single bar is stone-flagged and inviting, with old settles, coaching-lamps and maps giving warmth to the grey stone. The Lamb is also an hotel these days, and the charming residents' lounge takes up the remaining frontage on Sheep Street. At one time it had its own brewery next door and although local beer is still supplied The Lamb today is a free house selling mainly Flowers' and Worthington beers.

The garden is a sheer delight in summer. Gently sloping lawns are bordered by magnificent rose-beds, and the whole atmosphere is one of perfect peace and quiet.

Burford is often described as being a good centre for exploring the Cotswolds. This may well be true, but starting at The Lamb and ending at the little stone bridge over the Windrush, Burford itself is worth a thorough exploration before journeying farther afield.

CHARLBURY

The Bell

Brewer Ind Coope. *Bedrooms* 6. *Food* Restaurant. *Special drinks* Benskin's Bitter. *Route* B4437. *Nearest station* Charlbury. *Telephone* Charlbury 278.

Two miles north of Woodstock on the A34 a road branches left to Charlbury and Shipton-under-Wychwood. It seems an unfrequented road, running over high ground with vistas of cornfields, farms and small woods. This is a truly agricultural area, and is no doubt the reason for Charlbury's existence, situated as it is midway between the bigger market-towns of Chipping Norton and Witney.

The Bell is in Church Street, at the Woodstock end of the town. It is an enchanting pub, stone fronted in Georgian times but with the date of the original building, 1700, carved in the stonework.

The gardens at the back drop away dramatically. From the front are views of the rolling Oxfordshire countryside, for here we are high above the Evenlode and the great forest of Wychwood beyond.

As is usual in Oxfordshire it is no surprise to find the floors stone-flagged. The bar has a most attractive window-seat and a big fireplace on which rests an ancient gun-rack. This was, in its time, a posting-inn, and on display is the old Inland Revenue plate giving authority for this function.

Ind Coope's supply the beer at The Bell, and supply it mainly as Benskin's bitter! There is no mild.

Although Charlbury may seem today a sleepy little place it has had its moments. The great house in Cornbury Park was the home of the Earl of Leicester, favourite of Queen Elizabeth, who came there often. Charlbury is unlikely to have had much sleep on those occasions.

CHINNOR

The Crown

Brewer Aylesbury Brewery Co. *Food* Snacks. *Special drinks* Ind Coope's Bitter and Mild, Draught Guinness, Watney's Red Barrel. *Route* B4009. *Nearest station* Chinnor. *Telephone* Kingston Blount 244.

At the foot of the Chiltern Hills, between Princes Risborough and the A40, lies the village of Chinnor. It is dominated by the cement-works on the road to Bledlow, and though not a place of much beauty has at least one attractive inn. This is The Crown, an old half-timbered coaching-inn now belonging to the Aylesbury Brewery Company, standing at the cross-roads in the centre of the village.

Internally it remains practically untouched, though some years back an adjoining cottage was incorporated into the saloon-bar, revealing a massive curved Elizabethan fireplace which is now a pleasant feature of the room. The low ceilings and black rafters preserve the feeling of age without being oppressive, and the tiny public-bar is in the same tradition, though with a modern fireplace which also manages to look ancient.

Two hundred years ago the rector of Chinnor decided, as many a cleric has done since, to bring the church to the inn. His visits to The Crown became so frequent and so enjoyable that after a time he was rarely to be found in church, and the services were finally transferred to the saloon-bar of the inn.

Unfortunately this pleasant mixture of the temporal and spiritual no longer pertains, although there *are* pubs which hold a Harvest Festival service each year on the premises. Perhaps The Crown might do this one day—it has at least a precedent for it—and a name for good 'service'.

CHINNOR

Sir Charles Napier   SPRIGGS ALLEY

Free House. Food Snacks. *Special drinks* Ind Coope's Bitter and Mild, Watney's Red Barrel. *Route* 2 miles from A40 at Stokenchurch. *Nearest station* Chinnor. *Telephone* Radnage 3271.

Spriggs Alley or Spriggs Holly? The matter has been debated for generations by the inhabitants of this rural and remote area lying just within the Oxfordshire border between Chinnor and Stokenchurch. Certainly at one time this spot, high up in the Chilterns, was noted for its holly, and the pleasantly named Venus Wood near by might also indicate the presence of mistletoe.

The Sir Charles Napier has been a pub since the seventeenth century. As a free house it had not the advantages of being under the wing of a brewery, and remained for many years a derelict sort of place until it finally closed down.

Today it belongs to a local landowner who has extended and renovated it, and a very cosy and pleasant place it is. With so much timber available it is not surprising that this has been used almost exclusively in the improvements, and the saloon-bar, virtually rebuilt by the owner, shows what can be done without professional assistance by someone who knows his material.

There is a huge car-park, and at the back of this lies a caravan camping-site with wonderful views towards Stokenchurch and the Thames Valley.

There should never be any shortage of fuel in the Sir Charles Napier. For many years the landlord had the privilege of having as much free timber as he could use from the surrounding woods. Though snacks are provided, faggots are not on the menu.

CHIPPING NORTON

The Fox

Brewer Ind Coope. *Food* Restaurant. *Special drinks* Benskin's Beers, Draught Double Diamond. *Route* A44. *Nearest station* Chipping Norton. *Telephone* Chipping Norton 158.

The sloping car-park in the centre of Chipping Norton is an unexpected hazard to the visitor newly arrived in this pleasant town. Perhaps it is something to do with the fact that Norton is higher than any other town in Oxfordshire, or perhaps it is just to give the townsfolk something to talk about. For it is said that nothing of any importance has ever happened here, except for the famous scandal in the seventeenth century when Bishop

Juxon's hounds chased the hare through the sacred precincts of the churchyard.

But, of course, as in all small towns things do go on, though they may never get into the guide-books. Things which are talked about in the shops, and in the pubs, and wherever the locals gather.

One of these places is The Fox, hiding coyly behind the Market Hall at the end of the car-park. The saloon-bar is intimate, with a friendly atmosphere which makes the visitor feel he has lived in Chipping Norton all his life. There is a massive stone fireplace, and various items of Victoriana about the place which can be bought. But these are minor items compared with the sociable atmosphere of the bar itself. The small curved counter pulls one into the general conversation, and the long road ahead to Banbury or Worcester seems less and less attractive.

This is an Ind Coope pub, with Benskin's draught beer and Double Diamond waiting for you. And if you get so involved with local matters that your stay is unduly prolonged, there is also plenty of food.

CHISELHAMPTON

The Coach and Horses

Brewer Courage. *Bedrooms* 2. *Food* Snacks. *Route* B480 Oxford–Watlington. *Nearest station* Morris Cowley. *Telephone* Stadhampton 255.

The country between Dorchester, on the Oxford to Henley road (A423), and the A40 north of it, is one of open arable land with few villages. Through it wanders the little River Thame, touching only three roads in this seven-mile stretch.

Chiselhampton, where the river meets the Oxford to Watlington road, is a tiny village almost lost in this rural area. But The Coach and Horses, a handsome Tudor inn near the little bridge, keeps it firmly on the map. The whitewashed walls, dormer windows and massive sign stand out in this flat countryside and immediately claim the attention of the passer-by.

The true age of The Coach and Horses can be seen inside. In the cosy lounge a dividing wall has been partially demolished, but the supporting beams have been left intact with great effect.

24

The Coach and Horses

Courage own this pub, and a great feature is made of the fact that the beer is all 'from the wood'. The great barrels can be seen in the cellar, just behind the bar, and there is a plentiful supply of snacks.

Being only seven miles from Oxford, The Coach and Horses attracts not only the traveller on the road but has a steady clientèle from the city. The conversation is varied—and stimulating. A magnificent grand-piano in the lounge, now rarely played, recalls tales of music and musicians. And if the visitor happens to be interested in railways, and the Great Western in particular, his stay is quite likely to be very prolonged.

CHRISTMAS COMMON

The Fox and Hounds

Brewer Henley Brewery Co. *Food* Snacks. *Route* B481 Nettlebed–Stokenchurch. *Telephone* Watlington 495.

There are several places where the boundary between two counties follows the line of some definite geographical feature. We can tell immediately, by looking at the scenery, which county we are in. From a point on the Oxford side of Stokenchurch, at the top of Aston Hill, the county boundary runs along the ridge of the Chilterns as they drop to the Thames at Henley. There is just room for a lane to run between the boundary and the sharp edge of the hills, and along this road lies Christmas Common, remote and beautiful, looking down on to Watlington and the Oxfordshire plain below.

The Fox and Hounds is a little old country pub standing back from the road with a horse-pond in front. It has looked like this for a very, very long time.

The biggest and most-used room is the public-bar, the saloon being more or less an annexe, though a bright and cheerful one. The pub belongs to the Henley Brewery Company who have decided, very wisely, not to tamper with it or add anything to the character it already has.

The Christmas Day truce of the First World War in 1914 had a precedent here three hundred years before. Cromwell's men held Watlington, down below, the Royalists held the heights of the Chilterns. On Christmas Day in 1643 the opposing troops decided to have a rest. They met on the common, and perhaps had a drink together in The Fox and Hounds. At any rate the place has been called Christmas Common ever since, and will certainly never be called anything else.

CROWELL

The Catherine Wheel

Brewer Aylesbury Brewery Co. *Food* Meals served in saloon-bar. *Special drinks* Inde Coope's Bitter and Mild, Draught Guinness, Watney's Red Barrel. *Route* B4009 Watlington–Chinnor. *Telephone* Kingston Blount 431.

After most of Crowell was burnt down in 1759 The Catherine Wheel was one of the first buildings to rise from the ashes to begin a new lease of life as the village inn. This it did under the able direction of a Mistress Floyd. This cheerful and energetic body left as a legacy the imprint of her cheerfulness on this pub, now one of the houses of the Aylesbury Brewery Company.

26

It lies on rising ground just north of the A40, on the Chinnor to Watlington road. The situation is attractive for a start, looking across the village to the flat Oxfordshire plain on one side with the heights of the Chilterns as a back-drop behind.

The main bar is at the back of the building and seems so much a part of the place that it is difficult to realise that it is, in fact, a lean-to added on at some time in the past, and at one time housing sheep and goats. The comfortable atmosphere in this room is due in a very great extent to the old chairs, settles and other furniture which have obviously been chosen with great care. A smaller room at the front of the building also contains some interesting pieces, notably a copy of the chair used by John Bunyan in Bedford gaol. The fact that Bunyan regularly played the flute in prison, but no flute could ever be found in his cell, perplexed his custodians a great deal. The answer was in the chair, one of the struts being a flute cunningly incorporated into the design.

The atmosphere of The Catherine Wheel has just the right amount of eccentricity to ensure its not being forgotten. This extends even to the conveniences, where some bricks have been removed at eye-level allowing one to gaze straight into the churchyard and the many grave-stones visible. This may be intended as a sobering reminder of how finite we all are. On the other hand it may equally well be a tactful suggestion to get another pint down quickly, before the Last Trumpet calls.

DEDDINGTON

The Unicorn

Brewer Hunt Edmunds. *Food* Snacks. *Route* A423 Oxford–Banbury. *Nearest station* Banbury. *Telephone* Deddington 266.

'Drunken Deddington' it was once called—but that was a long time ago. Certainly Deddington seems sober enough today, even a little prim. It straddles the main road from Oxford to Banbury about six miles south of the latter, and, like Banbury, most of it lies off the main road hidden from view.

Part of its primness stems from its grouping round the large and airy market-place dominated by the famous church, although it is the church, or at least the church bells, which earned Deddington its epithet. The earlier tower fell down in 1635 and the bells were left lying on the ground. The business-like inhabitants of Deddington sold them for cannon-balls, and celebrated in true country fashion.

No doubt The Unicorn, one of the two inns in the market-place, made its own contribution to the revelries, and probably started a fund for bigger and better church bells! At any rate the church today has eight bells but so far The Unicorn seems to be able to satisfy the thirsts of its customers without recourse to any further melting-down of church property.

There is only one bar in this old inn, but it is a large one. There is the usual smoke-room, that favourite adjunct of Oxfordshire pubs, but no saloon. Parking is no problem here—the entire market-place is at one's disposal.

The front of this Hunt Edmunds pub is Georgian, of white stone in keeping with the rest of Deddington, and contributing to the air of primness. No doubt this impression is inaccurate—as inaccurate, in fact, as the 'drunken' epithet Deddington earned for itself so long ago.

DORCHESTER-ON-THAMES

The George Hotel

Free House. Bedrooms 8. *Food* Restaurant. *Special drinks* Morland's Bitter, Whitbread's Tankard. *Route* A423 Wallingford–Oxford. *Nearest station* Abingdon. *Telephone* Warborough 404.

The visitor to Dorchester today will find it difficult to believe that this little Thames-side village was once a city. True, this was a long time ago—a thousand years, in fact, when it was the cathedral city of Mercia about the year 900. Not only did it have a cathedral, but an abbey, a monastery and seven other churches besides. Today the great Abbey alone remains, and opposite stands The George. Not, of course, that The George is as old as the Abbey, though it stands on the site of the original abbey hospice. It dates from 1450 and is certainly one of the oldest inns in the country. It is also one of the very few inns left with the original galleries over the yard, and to wander around outside this place gives a hint of what might be expected within.

28

The galleries lead to the original 'Travellers' Lodgings' and are reached by a picturesque staircase from the yard. Most of the rooms in The George are half-timbered, but their loftiness is an unusual feature in a building of such age.

The bar itself is not very large, with a character in keeping with the rest of the building, low fireside benches and massive blackened beams.

But it is the dining-room which is one of the chief glories of The George. Here the beams and rafters soar to the roof like some great cathedral, and at the end of the room the tall brick chimney vanishes into the darkness high up above the roaring fire. Small wonder that this is considered to be one of the finest examples of mediaeval domestic architecture in England.

The George has sheltered many travellers on the Oxford to London road, probably one of the most illustrious being Sarah, Duchess of Marlborough when travelling from Woodstock. But its long career is by no means over, and many future travellers will no doubt come to marvel at the wonder of it all, and to explore this once great city.

DUCKLINGTON

The Bell

Brewer Courage. *Food* Snacks. *Route* A415 Witney–Abingdon. *Nearest station* Witney. *Telephone* Witney 514.

South of Witney the road to Newbridge and the county boundary follows the twisting course of the Windrush River. Less than two miles from the centre of Witney, flanked by a series of watery ditches, stands the village of Ducklington.

Though small it has everything a village ought to have. There is a fifteenth-century church, village pond, two pubs and a shop.

The Bell lies well back from the road on the Newbridge side of the village. It presents the customary stone front of Oxfordshire buildings, but an odd feature is the flight of steps leading down into the two bars. The little lounge-bar on the right is uninspiring, and used mainly at week-ends. The bar on the left, bigger and with a great stone fireplace, is where the locals gather for darts and dominoes.

It is a truism that a pub takes its character mainly from the landlord and his customers. The building itself may be attractive, but horse-brasses and inglenooks alone contribute little to the conversation. But in this Courage house the friendly atmosphere is apparent immediately, and the stranger is drawn into the chatter and made to feel at home with remarkable speed.

The parish church of St Bartholomew has a ring of six bells, and no doubt these are responsible for the name of this inn. As an additional reminder the public-bar contains a delightful collection of tiny bells of varying sizes and varying tones, which are used to signal the approach of 'Time'. Few pubs have thought of such a harmonious way of ejecting their customers.

EYNSHAM

The Red Lion

Brewer Morrell. *Food* Snacks. *Special drinks* Draught Light Ale, Varsity Keg Bitter. *Route* A4141 Witney–Oxford. *Nearest station* Eynsham. *Telephone* Eynsham 228.

White-fronted, with neat wooden palings, The Red Lion stands in the old market-place next to the eleventh-century church. Indeed, it is almost part of the church, and certainly as old, as part of the churchyard wall is incorporated into the ancient pig-sties of the inn, at the bottom of the garden.

It is a Morrell pub, and if you are interested in football, dominoes or darts, then this is the place for you. It is very much a 'local', with none of the aloofness occasionally found in country inns, where the presence of a stranger cuts conversation like a knife and the visitor is given the treatment normally reserved for one of the Borgias. In The Red Lion it is impossible not to be drawn into the conversation, and almost certainly you will be playing darts or dominoes before very long.

The snug saloon-bar has an unusual décor of old oil-lamps. Not only are they old, but they are used for lighting and give a most pleasant effect to this charming room. From the main beam hangs a collection of china mugs, and a showcase holds various cups won by the football team.

One odd thing about The Red Lion is that you cannot buy ordinary

30

raught bitter. Varsity Keg Bitter is available, but ordinary beer comes as raught light. Whatever the virtues of this brew it certainly seems to breed rowess on the field of sport if the cups are anything to go by.

Across the square from The Red Lion stands a rather forbidding-looking one building with massive iron gates. This was the lock-up in former days, nd is now the public library and part of the Council Offices.

This is a pity in a way. It would be nice to see a customer of The Red Lion rcing the iron bars apart with his bare hands, suitably fortified with raught light.

GODSTOW

The Trout

Brewer Charrington. *Food* Restaurant. *Route* 1 mile off A40 (Oxford By-Pass). *Nearest station* Oxford. *Telephone* Oxford 54485.

A mile-and-a-half upstream from Oxford lies Godstow. The Trout, on the iver-bank, has ministered to generations of undergraduates, and even before the first colleges of the university began to be built, was supplying efreshment to travellers as the guest-house of the ancient nunnery. Many re the legends surrounding this historic place. The fair young Rosamund, oved by Henry II, is said to have been buried here, poisoned by the jealous queen. At the dissolution of the monasteries the nunnery was reduced to uins, but the guest-house was enlarged with the broken stone from the cloisters, and continued its career as a riverside inn.

But to Oxford students The Trout means the river, and boating. It means he bridge and the weir, the stone terrace bordering the river, the view back across Port Meadow to the 'dreaming spires' of the university town. It was on river-trips from Oxford to Godstow and back that Lewis Carroll first old of Alice, inventing the story as he went along, to the delight of his young passengers. Like all good pubs The Trout moves with the times, but yet remains a most delightful place and still as popular as it has always been. The several bars are normally crowded, and it is a relief to take one's drink to the river-bank on a summer evening, or sit on the stone terrace as the sun sinks, to ponder on the sights The Trout has seen in its long and eventful

The Trou

history. It is, as ever, the meeting-place of countrymen and city-dwellers,
of young and of old, and more than ever in these times, of various nation-
alities. When Matthew Arnold's Scholar Gipsy was glimpsed 'above
Godstow Bridge' The Trout was already old, and generations yet to come
will savour its delights and look back on it with nostalgia.

GORING-ON-THAMES

Ye Olde Leatherne Bottel

Free House. Bedrooms 3. *Food* Restaurant. *Special drinks* Brakspear's Henley
Brewery P.A., Whitbread's Tankard, Flower's Keg, Watney's Red Barrel.
Route B4009 Goring–Newnham. *Nearest station* Goring and Streatley.
Telephone Goring 2667.

Both Goring and the Thames are fairly easily identifiable spots. It is therefore
with mounting surprise and frustration that the would-be visitor to this old

riverside inn discovers just how elusive it can be. True, the landlord will present you with a card bearing full instruction on how to get there—but as this is after you have arrived it is largely pointless.

From Goring and Streatley station the road runs up to Crowmarsh (B4009). A mile along this road the second turning to the left is marked 'bridle-path only'. Don't let this put you off, for it is three hundred yards down this lane that the Leatherne Bottel lies. The lane itself ends rather dramatically almost on the roof of the inn, and a tortuous extension winds down to the river-bank and the car-park. But the journey is very worth while. Here the river is wide, and the long lasher with the view of the Berkshire bank and Streatley Hill combine to make it one of the most attractive situations on the Thames.

The licence of the Leatherne Bottel, which is a free house, goes back at least four hundred years. There is no public-bar, most of the ground-floor being given over to the charming and picturesque lounge and the dining-room. There is a massive chimney-piece, a collection of horse-brasses, warming-pans and other brass accoutrements, and a small curved bar.

There is also said to be an ancient well producing health-giving waters, but most customers settle for the Red Barrel or Whitbread Tankard and feel all the better for it.

HENLEY-ON-THAMES

The Angel Hotel

Brewer Henley Brewery Co. *Food* Restaurant open to 10 p.m., teas on river terrace. *Special drinks* Whitbread's Tankard. *Route* A423. *Nearest station* Henley-on-Thames. *Telephone* Henley-on-Thames 110.

Henley is famous for at least two things—glassware and the Regatta. The glass was an importation from Flintshire in the seventeenth century, the Regatta an importation from Oxford in the nineteenth. But perhaps that is not quite fair. The Regatta is now so much part of Henley that the race between Oxford and Cambridge in 1837, which is said to have started it all, is now almost forgotten. It is enough that Henley saw the possibilities of this affair and two years later, in 1839, started the long series of river races which today

33

The Angel Hotel

attracts entries from all over the world. The Angel will no doubt be familiar to many who have visited the town. It stands on the river-bank at the end of the bridge, a building of many storeys and of many levels. The two main bars, together with the handsome dining-room, are upstairs, and in the summer there is an additional 'Terrazzo' bar on the river-bank. This is devoted to teas, outside licensed hours, and a most delightful spot it is. The twisting stairs inside this old inn give it a special character, though the confusion of doors can give rise to occasional misunderstandings.

The Henley Brewery Company are at the helm, and the stores include quantities of food and Whitbread's Tankard.

HENLEY-ON-THAMES

The Bull   BELL STREET

Brewer Henley Brewery Co. *Food* Snacks. *Route* A423. *Nearest station* Henley-on-Thames. *Telephone* Henley-on-Thames 621.

In a town full of ancient and historic inns The Bull is probably the oldest, and certainly the most picturesque. The frontage on Bell Street, with its gables and overhanging first-floor make startling comparison with the chromium-and-glass of the modern shop-fronts lining this busy street.

The house belongs to the Henley Brewery Company and has been preserved by them with great care. There are massive timbers in the ancient archway which leads to the tiny saloon-bar, where the black beams seem to take up most of the available space.

It seems typical of the older pubs of Henley that a fine exterior hides a somewhat disappointing and cramped interior. But with newer buildings jostling on either side it is no doubt very difficult to make any drastic changes internally. In many instances, as here, the public-bar is at the front and is by far the biggest room. It is in the public that one can usually see the structure of the building and trace the various additions and alterations made during the centuries. Certainly, at The Bull, no attempt has been made to superimpose pseudo-antique ornamentation on the existing fabric. In the public it is unnecessary—and in the saloon there just isn't the room.

HENLEY-ON-THAMES

The Old White Hart

Brewer Henley Brewery Co. *Bedrooms* 10. *Food* Restaurant. *Route* A423. *Nearest station* Henley-on-Thames. *Telephone* Henley-on-Thames 103.

Coming up the busy street from Henley Bridge to the centre of the town one could easily miss The Old White Hart. It stands on the right, displaying a narrow stone-and-timber front which has obviously been restored, and an arch. And it is the arch which is the key to this delightful inn, and leads to a world far remote from the bustling Henley of today.

The half-timbered buildings, the rare, overhanging galleries looking on to the yard seem unaffected by the changes outside. Here, five hundred years ago, the citizens of the town thronged to watch the bear-baiting and cock-fighting, crowding into the yard from the street, whilst the privileged looked on from the galleries above. It takes little imagination to visualise the scene, for here is a corner of Tudor England still intact, and only a few feet away from the twentieth century.

Immediately behind the façade of The Old White Hart is the public-bar, a lofty room of black beams and yellow shining plaster. The saloon-bar and dining-room are reached from the yard and though, perhaps, not quite so genuinely evocative of a past age as the yard are nevertheless venerable and comfortable.

This is a rambling building, of twisted staircases and winding corridors. The dining-room is reached by a short passage from the saloon-bar, and it is all in character that quite unexpectedly one finds a little room in between, in addition. This, again unexpectedly, houses a small exhibition of paintings by a local artist, all of which are for sale.

Despite the many attractions of The Old White Hart one must not lose sight of the beer, which is provided by the Henley Brewery. No doubt this obliging company would provide bear-baiting as well, if the demand warranted it.

HENLEY-ON-THAMES

The Walnut Tree FAWLEY

Brewer Henley Brewery Co. *Food* Snacks. *Route* 2 miles north of A4155 (Henley–Marlow). *Nearest station* Henley-on-Thames. *Telephone* Turville Heath 360.

About two miles due north of Henley the tiny village of Fawley stands more or less on the county boundary between Oxfordshire and Buckinghamshire. The little lanes around it lead nowhere in particular but seem to trail off and lose themselves in the woody heights that mark the beginning of the Chilterns. The Walnut Tree is a fairly new inn, and seems of a size out of all proportion to the size of the village. Built in 1958 by the Henley Brewery Company, it is a bright and comfortable place and although seemingly remote it attracts a good deal of trade from Henley and the district around.

At one time there was talk of cutting a new road from Nettlebed, by-passing Henley and joining up with the Marlow road near Hambleden. Unfortunately the planners changed their minds, but in the meantime the new pub had been built to cope with the traffic which was expected through Fawley, on the line of the new road.

Nevertheless it is a pleasant change to find a village pub with all the amenities of a larger place, and The Walnut Tree has much to commend it. There is plenty of room for parking, a very large garden, and it is 540 feet up, if you like statistics.

That it enjoys more custom than one might expect is proved by some of the decorations in the saloon-bar. There is a wonderful collection of foreign tiles contributed by customers, some interesting modern tapestry, and very good elm tables and chairs made by local craftsmen. The beer is from the wood, and wine is sold by the glass.

KINGHAM

The Langston Arms

Free House. Food Snacks. *Special drinks* Draught Bass, Hunt Edmunds' Best Bitter, Flowers' I.P.A., Bitter, Mitchell & Butler's Mild, Whitbread's Tankard, Worthington E. Keg. *Route* B4450 Stow-on-the-Wold–Chipping Norton. *Nearest station* Kingham. *Telephone* Kingham 209.

Despite the enthusiasm for the railways shown by the town-dweller during the great era of expansion, many country towns and villages protested violently at this intrusion into their lives and the desecration of the countryside. The railways were forced to go round, and it followed that if a station was being provided this would be, inevitably, some distance from the village. This frustrating arrangement is seen up and down the country, but in the age of swift road transport is less frustrating than it was.

The line connecting Chipping Norton, in Oxfordshire, with Stow-on-the-Wold in Worcestershire serves one village only in between—Kingham. Even so it manages to avoid it by nearly two miles, providing a station that distance from the village, almost on the county boundary. A hundred years ago, not long after the railway came to these parts, the local squire Langston decided this arrangement was not very satisfactory for his friends who came for shooting-parties at week-ends. The answer was to build a huge hunting-lodge near the station, complete with stables, outhouses and all the trappings which marked Victorian opulence.

Today this monstrous example of mid-Victorian architecture is The

Langston Arms. It stands by the roadside, bleak and forbidding, the very antithesis of the cosy country pub we have come to love so well.

But this book does not deal entirely with cosy country pubs. Any pub that is different is worthy of inclusion—and The Langston Arms is certainly different. Inside, the atmosphere is still 'decayed Victorian', but compared with the outside rather more sociable. It is a free house, with a good range of beers on tap, and the bar has, by way of decoration, various hunting-daggers and a Boer War rifle.

It also has what appears to be a perfectly genuine ghost, a rare pheno-menon in a trade where ghost stories of doubtful authenticity are carefully kept alive by publicity-minded licensees. This apparition manifests itself as the faintly luminous outline of a female, and appears at irregular intervals, by night or by day. It has appeared several days running, or may disappear for weeks at a time. It has been seen by locals when the pub is full, gliding along behind the counter and vanishing straight through a massive mahogany fitting. It does no harm, it seems, although a previous landlord decided to have it exorcised. The expert cleric who came to perform this function carried out some preliminary tests, pronounced it a benevolent spirit, and refused to give it the full treatment normally reserved for poltergeists and such unfriendly phenomena. So there it remains—contributing one more unusual facet to this unusual pub, and having the distinction of being probably the only Victorian ghost on Victorian licensed premises. Not even the locals can provide a clue to its existence. Perhaps Squire Langston or one of his sporty friends 'dun 'er wrong'—or perhaps she sheltered in the lodge after missing her train, and has never found the way out! But she is there, even if she does not run to a time-table, and your chance of seeing her is as good as the next customer's.

MARSTON FERRY

The Victoria Arms

Free House. Food Snacks. *Special drinks* Whitbread's Bitter or Mild, Younger's Bitter and Scotch Ale, Flowers' Keg, Draught Guinness. *Route* A40. *Nearest station* Oxford. *Telephone* Oxford 48386.

The unlovely village of Marston lies just south of the northern by-pass two miles from the Headington roundabout. It is a flat and damp part of Oxford, and had a brief moment of fame when Cromwell was besieging the city and made the village his headquarters. Fairfax received the surrender of Oxford here, a decisive event in the history of the Civil War.

Marston lies about half a mile from the River Cherwell, the second of the two rivers which encompass the city and eventually join just south of it. The Victoria Arms is a riverside pub reached by a track across the fields, and adjoining a ferry which has been functioning on the spot since the twelfth century.

The building itself is old, but has been a pub only since the early nineteenth century. Many pubs and inns have been named after that formidable ruler, but it is rare to find a sign depicting her, as here, as a young woman at the time of her marriage.

The Victoria Arms is a free house and has recently been given an internal face-lift, if that is not a contradiction in terms. It was derelict and untenanted for three years after a disastrous fire but is now very much back in the picture. Most features of the old building have been kept, including the enormous bread-oven in the saloon-bar, and its site on the river-bank well away from the village makes it an attractive place for the explorer. It also brings home very vividly the realisation that the university buildings and the area normally seen by tourists is only a very small part of the sprawling conglomeration which is the Oxford of today.

MILTON COMMON

The Three Pigeons

Brewer Ind Coope. *Food* Snack-bar. *Special drinks* Draught Cider, Cornish Mead. *Route* A40. *Nearest station* Thame. *Telephone* Great Milton 247.

On the busy A40 half-way between Tetsworth and Wheatley, The Three Pigeons stands on the site of an ancient gallows. It is a pleasant-looking pub with a good and easily accessible car-park, and is a useful stop for the hurried traveller to or from Oxford. Great importance is laid on quick service, particularly in respect of food, but it is, at the same time, a pleasant place to linger and rest from the nerve-wracking effort of driving.

It is an Ind Coope pub, with public- and saloon-bars, both quite large, and a snack-bar incorporated in the latter.

Travellers are notoriously thirsty people, and The Three Pigeons, recognising this, boasts no fewer than sixty different brands of whisky, and also serves draught cider and Cornish mead.

Mead was, of course, a favourite drink of the Ancient Britons though not, as many imagine, their staple diet. This was milk, which probably accounts for the fact that they became Ancient, the mead being reserved for special occasions such as weddings. Mead is made from honey—the wedding celebrations lasted a lunar month, hence the expression 'honey-moon'.

With this wealth of liquid refreshment available The Three Pigeons is a popular stop for many. And as if the amount of alcohol on the premises still does not give the traveller sufficient choice there is a ready alternative. There is a spring in the cellar—and water in unlimited quantity.

MINSTER LOVELL

The Old Swan

Free House. Bedrooms 9. *Food* Restaurant. *Special drinks* Draught Double Diamond, Watney's Red Barrel. *Route* near A40. *Nearest station* Witney. *Telephone* Asthall Leigh 614.

Two miles from Witney on the Gloucester side a finger-post points the way to Minster Lovell. The road, suddenly quiet and peaceful after the roar of the heavy lorries grinding their way to South Wales, drops down through a wood, crosses the tiny River Windrush and enters this most beautiful of Cotswold villages.

The Old Swan is practically the first building—a mixture of stone and half-timbering (rare in these parts) and dating from the fifteenth century. Creeper-covered, with its dormer windows, flagstone pavement surrounding and elm benches outside it seems as remote and peaceful as if the Windrush were not a little river but a vast sea separating it from the busy world on the hill.

But this is the atmosphere of the whole of the village, and indeed of most of the villages on this river. Yet apart from its beauty, Minster Lovell is

40

famous for the somewhat gruesome story perpetuated in *The Mistletoe Bough* in which a young bride, playing hide-and-seek on her wedding-night, locked herself in an old chest from which she found it impossible to escape. The old home of the Lovells, at which this incident occurred, is now a ruin, but a lovely one. Late in the fifteenth century Francis Lovell hid in a secret room known only to himself and a servant, to escape his pursuers. The servant died, and Francis was not seen again until 1718—a bony shadow of his former self with the skeleton of a dog at his feet.

Apart from these two dramatic incidents little seems to have happened in Minster Lovell through the years. The visitor to The Old Swan may be intrigued by the twisting staircases and unexpected rooms and may explore in safety. The landlord knows about all of them.

NEWBRIDGE

The Rose Revived

Brewer Morland. *Bedrooms* 7. *Food* Restaurant. *Route* A415 Witney–Abingdon. *Nearest station* Witney. *Telephone* Standlake 221.

Despite its name Newbridge marks the site of one of the oldest of Thames bridges. It is here that the little Windrush joins its big brother, both having wandered far and wide since leaving their native Gloucestershire.

The Rose Revived is a Morland inn built on the site of a previous hostelry called The Rose. This accounts for the 'Revived' part of the name, and indeed the revision has been complete and successful.

It stands on the river-bank by the old bridge, in an attractive setting. Internally the design is one of mellow comfort, and although comparatively new the small bar with its wooden roof and the various pieces of good antique furniture make it one of the most pleasant pubs in the area.

As might be expected in a pub of this type, the public-bar has been largely left to its own devices. It contains, however, a monumental chimney-piece which is worth seeing.

The Rose Revived has a good name for food, and is a very popular place at all times of the year. It is fortunate in having a large car-park, suitable for very large cars, and thus accommodating with the greatest of ease the affluent types who congregate there. In the summer many come by boat from Oxford, looking studiedly nautical and with a decided list to port. But whichever way you arrive you will enjoy The Rose Revived—and probably wish that more village inns could be 'revived' with such success.

OXFORD

The Bear Inn ALFRED STREET

Brewer Ind Coope. *Food* Snack-bar. *Special drinks* 'Schooners' of sherry. *Nearest station* Oxford. *Telephone* Oxford 44680.

In the angle formed by the High Street and St Aldates stands The Bear, at the junction of Alfred Street and Blue Boar Street. It is a little pub, part of a much larger building which extended most of the way up Alfred Street in the seventeenth century. Although in the centre of the City of Oxford, The Bear looks more like a country pub than a city tavern. The whitewashed walls, the hanging baskets of geraniums and the swinging sign all combine to give it a rural atmosphere. In fact it has seen a great deal of Oxford history and in 1573 the landlord, one Anthony Hall, was elected Mayor of the city. But not all landlords were so illustrious or fortunate. Thomas Hearn, the Oxford diarist, recounts how in 1733 the daughter of the landlord was delivered of child, much to the concern of the doting parents. 'She lays it' he says, 'to one Rigby, a Gentleman of Wadham, to whom she says she is married, what no one believes.'

The Bear is known all over the world, and for many things. Probably its main claim to fame rests in the fantastic collection of ties which adorn the walls in hundreds. Only a small piece of the tie is taken, and this only with the owner's consent, the ceremony being performed with an enormous pair of ceremonial scissors, with drinks 'on the house' to follow. They are arranged in show-cases round the walls, each signed by the donor, and many are the famous names inscribed.

The Bear is small, and usually crowded. During term it is a favourite with undergraduates, the vacation bringing visitors and sightseers from almost every country in the world. One day, perhaps, it will fall a victim to road-widening and town-planning, but that is likely to be a very long time head. At least, when it does happen, no doubt The Bear will have even more 'ties' with the past than it has today.

OXFORD

Forte's Motor Lodge
WOODSTOCK ROAD

Free House. Bedrooms 60. *Food* Restaurant and snack-bar. *Special drinks* Draught Double Diamond. *Route* A34. *Nearest station* Oxford. *Telephone* Oxford 54301.

On the second roundabout from Oxford on the Woodstock road stands a series of modern buildings which seems far removed from any normal village pub. This is an example of the latest development in 'motels', a ghastly word which Forte's quite rightly avoid, substituting the more euphonious 'motor lodge'. As its name implies there is everything for the motorist here. Accommodation, garages, petrol-pumps, snack-bar and dining-room, even a gift-shop. But even if you arrive on foot (an unlikely possibility) and have no vehicle to be watered and fed, you can still use the bar and stand in wonder at the lush décor and comfortable surroundings provided by this amazing organisation.

The car-park holds three hundred cars, and there are sixty bedrooms all with television (you don't *have* to switch on). The snack-bar is open twenty-four hours a day, the drinking-bar open only the 'permitted hours' normal to the county of Oxfordshire. This infuriating arrangement, whilst tolerated by the British, is a source of great mystery to the visiting foreigner, accustomed to being allowed to slake his thirst without Government permission.

However, having got as far inland as Oxford no doubt he is becoming acclimatised to the British and their way of life. If not he may well throw himself into the superb swimming-pool of this extraordinary place, thoughtfully provided by an efficient management.

OXFORD

The Friar Bacon
CUTSLOW

Brewer Morrell. *Food* Snacks. *Route* A40. *Nearest station* Oxford. *Telephone* Oxford 58365.

43

Travelling westwards along the northern by-pass of the City of Oxford the three-mile stretch from the Headington roundabout to the junction with the Banbury road always seems endless. A sign that you have nearly accomplished the run is the sight of The Friar Bacon on the left, a welcome excuse to get out of the traffic and have a breather in the car-park even if the hour prohibits anything stronger inside.

This is a large pub, as befits its situation on a by-pass, with a seeming complexity of bars. It stands on a corner, one ear cocked towards the housing-estate from which it draws its regular trade, the other directed towards the passing flow of motorists. There are at least four bars, but by far the largest is the saloon which takes up most of the centre of the building. A small and attractive lounge is on one side, the public-bar and tap-room on the other. This is a Morrell house, and was built in 1920.

The curious name refers to Roger Bacon, Franciscan friar and man of learning in the thirteenth century, so before his time that his reputation as a dabbler in the black arts still persists. He is reputed to have lived in an Oxford inn known as The Blue Boar whose licence, when eventually demolished, became available for the new hostelry on the by-pass.

Though the licence was transferred, the name was not. It is, perhaps, not so odd after all that a comparatively modern pub on a busy main road should commemorate a man who was 'ultra-modern' in his time and who, in an age when travel was difficult and dangerous, commuted regularly between London and Paris!

OXFORD

The Golden Cross   OFF THE CORNMARKET

Free House. Bedrooms 33. *Food* Restaurant. *Special drinks* Draught Bass, Ind Coope's Bitter, Draught Double Diamond. *Nearest station* Oxford. *Telephone* Oxford 42391.

The march of progress in many of our big cities has too often resulted in the disappearance of beautiful and ancient buildings. At worst the disappearance is permanent, and demolition complete. But sometimes the building is spared, the planners hold back, and a way is found to preserve a building and at the same time carry out the improvements the town needs.

The Golden Cross is in this category. For three hundred years a coaching-inn it once presented its half-timbered front to the traveller entering Oxford on the Woodstock road. Today it is invisible from the street and is reached by a little alley off the Cornmarket just opposite Woolworths. But what a find it is! And what a mixture of architectural styles. On one side stands the oldest part of the inn, the many dormers, Tudor timbers and jutting windows with their gay flower-boxes making one catch the breath with their beauty. Across the yard is a Georgian 'improvement' covering the original front with white stone, widening the arch and inserting a row of windows of severe symmetry. The inside of The Golden Cross is just as fascinating, and just as much a mixture. It continues as an inn, and the more

The Golden Cross

picturesque parts are on the upper floors. The large bar below is character
istic of its time but also caters for the present age without striking a wron
note in the process. Like most hotels it is a free house, untied to any on
brewer. This independence seems part of the personality of this fine ol
building which, with its roots in the past, still outwits the planners an
continues its tradition of distinguished service.

OXFORD

The Grapes QUEEN STREE

Brewer Morrell. *Nearest station* Oxford. *Telephone* Oxford 47372.

Right opposite the Playhouse stands The Grapes, a collector's piece if eve
there was one. It is a Morrell pub, a perfect example of the mirror-and
mahogany style of pub architecture now becoming all too rare. Th
entrance leads into a long corridor which, after passing the typical littl
cubicles displaying the stern elevations of the drinkers in the 'private' bar
terminates in a room which is only slightly larger than those passed, and i
the saloon. In its day The Grapes had its share of business from the 'pros' a
the theatre opposite. Today actors and actresses, and audiences too for tha
matter, seem to prefer the plushier atmosphere of the more modern pub
in the vicinity, and The Grapes is left with its memories—and its mahogany

But it is not a dull pub by any means. It sets out to cater for the type o
customer who still frequents it, and the *Oxford Mail*, in several editions, lie
on the bar for all to read at leisure. And leisure, these days, is becomin
almost as rare as mirrors and mahogany. Who can blame The Grapes i
by staying in the past, it manages to avoid the rush-and-tear of the present
There is always the *Oxford Mail* to remind you of the world outside.

OXFORD

The Red Lion GLOUCESTER GREEN

Brewer Ind Coope. *Food* Snack-bar. *Nearest station* Oxford. *Telephon*
Oxford 42100.

p the High Street and across the lights at Carfax and there is no mistaking
at 'gown' has given way to 'town'. Here is the Oxford of today, or part
f it, with the Playhouse, the cinema and the municipal car-park all in one
nall area. Behind the Playhouse, adjoining the car-park, is The Red Lion, a
rge and modern pub belonging to Ind Coope, with the sort of trade one
might expect in such a situation. It is a comfortable and extremely well-
ppointed place, with a long, curved bar terminating in a smaller bar
eserved for food. Signed photographs of famous actors who have trod the
layhouse boards adorn the walls, for this is a theatrical pub, and this in no
erogatory sense. The phrase 'having a quick one' is frequently more
ptimistic than accurate, but here at The Red Lion it really means what it
ays. They are used to dealing with actors gulping one down between
ppearances, with audiences dashing in during the interval, or with the
ommon herd knocking back a quick Scotch between buses, and they are
letermined none of them is going to miss their cue. The service is geared to
his sort of customer, though for those not in quite so much of a hurry there
re comfortable armchairs and tables from which one may drink and watch
he rest of the world flashing in and out. Or, of course, you can always lean
n the bar and listen as well as look. But don't expect to engage the barman
n close conversation—or you will be unpopular. He and his fellow-
workers move quicker than anybody in this place!

OXFORD

The Royal Oak   WOODSTOCK ROAD

Brewer Ind Coope. *Food* Grill-room. *Nearest station* Oxford. *Telephone*
Oxford 57403.

This tiny pub, on the right up the Woodstock road, has more character to
it than might be expected from the exterior. The saloon-bar is small, the
tap-room even smaller, yet the number of customers who manage to pack
into it must be seen to be believed. It is probably eighteenth century and has
a great deal of oak panelling about the rooms. This is relieved here and there
by stained-glass illustrations which include, for some unaccountable reason,
a portrait of Haydn. There is a wonderful collection of spirit-containers high

47

The Royal Oak

up on a shelf in the saloon, not only with the name of the contents inscribed but also carrying illustrations. Ornaments abound, though in the general melée it is difficult to appreciate anything less than six feet from the ground. Below this level, however, the ornaments are equally attractive and entertaining, consisting of a high proportion of women undergraduates, for several of the women's colleges are close at hand.

Ind Coope provide the beer and during term the University provides most of the customers. During the vac the ornaments and stained glass may be examined with a little more comfort—though much of the decoration will inevitably be missing.

OXFORD

The Turf Tavern

Brewer Ind Coope. *Bedrooms* 12. *Food* Snacks at bar, Restaurant. *Special drinks* Draught Cider. *Nearest station* Oxford. *Telephone* Oxford 43235.

The more hidden-away a pub is in Oxford the more sought-out it seems to be. There is a certain feeling of 'one-upmanship' in taking friends and relations to a place almost impossible to find and displaying that intimate knowledge of the city so dear to undergraduates.

The Turf Tavern is such a pub, tucked away in an alley just off Holywell in the angle formed by New College Lane. It is an ancient building of Oxfordshire stone, with a little garden floodlit at night, almost dwarfed by the taller buildings around.

At first sight the interior of the building seems to consist mainly of oak beams and ham sandwiches. This, of course, is an exaggeration—not all the sandwiches are ham. But the impression is certainly one of food, and food in vast quantities. Pies, pickles, sausages and salads are everywhere—but not for long. They disappear with such astonishing speed that one might be forgiven for thinking the customers had not eaten for a week. This pub is a favourite with undergraduates during Term. In the vacation they are replaced by foreign visitors and students, all appearing to be equally half-starved. To wash down the food there is Double Diamond and Red Barrel beer and draught cider, and a good selection of wine.

The correct address of The Turf is St Helen's Passage. This, as any undergraduate will tell you, must never, never be confused with Friar's Entry.

OXFORD

The Turl Tavern   TURL STREET

Free House. Bedrooms 47 (Mitre). *Food* Restaurant. *Special drinks* Worthington E, Younger's Scotch Ale, Double Diamond Keg, Whitbread's Tankard Keg, Mitchell & Butler's Brew Eleven and mild. *Nearest station* Oxford. *Telephone* Oxford 42335.

Narrow Turl Street runs from Broad Street to the High Street, the junction with the latter being marked by the Mitre Hotel on the corner. As an hotel, the Mitre is old and famous, and as might be expected with its wealth of experience manages to get the best of three worlds.

Behind the hotel, in Turl Street, a passage leads to what seems to be two

49

separate pubs. In fact this is The Turl Tavern, all part of the Mitre but apparently unconnected with that venerable institution.

The part of The Turl on the right is a long, spacious room, a favourite with undergraduates from Jesus and Exeter, both in Turl Street. It is an old building, and at one time may have formed part of the original courtyard of the Mitre.

The left-hand bar, and ostensibly a separate pub, is officially called the Tudor Bar and is used mainly by townsfolk. Inside the Mitre, again, there is the residents' lounge, though to find this one must come out of The Turl and enter by the front entrance in the High Street.

The combined drinking-space available under one roof must be the most extensive in the city. You have to hand it to the Mitre. Coping with both undergraduates and townsfolk alone is quite a feat, let alone ministering to the needs of the many visitors to this alcoholic area.

PEPPARD COMMON

The Dog

Brewer Simonds. *Food* Snacks. *Route* A4009 Reading–Nettlebed. *Nearest station* Reading. *Telephone* Rotherfield Greys 343.

The small area of the Oxfordshire Chilterns is quite unlike the Buckinghamshire part of this range of hills. The land is dropping towards the Thames, the beechwoods are giving way to open heathland and scrub, and the familiar chalk outcrops have largely vanished. From Reading the road to Nettlebed and Oxford runs due north, rising slightly to negotiate the southern tip of the Chilterns before descending to the Oxfordshire plain below.

Peppard Common is on this road, five miles north of Reading and still some three hundred feet above sea-level. It is a lovely spot for picnics in the summer, the great wide common ensuring a quick escape from the noise of traffic on the main road. The few buildings include The Dog, just off the road on the common, on the right from Reading. Originally a shop, it has had various ups-and-downs in its career before becoming a pub in 1740, when it was called variously The Dogg or The Talbot.

It is a Simonds house, and it is therefore not surprising to find the beer is still drawn from the wood cask. There is, of course, Tavern Keg in addition for those who prefer the pressurised brew.

The small saloon on the right is not particularly inspiring or decorative. It is cosy and comfortable enough, but without the character found in the public-bar. Here we find the building as it was, with great oak beams, an ingle-nook and solid wood settles. But whether you drink inside or outside it is a pleasant place from whatever view-point, and here, at least, there is no parking problem.

PISHILL

The Crown

Free House. Food Restaurant. *Special drinks* Worthington E, Morland's Bitter, Whitbread's Tankard, Watney's Red Barrel, Draught Guinness, Draught Cider. *Route* Off Nettlebed–Watlington road. *Nearest station* Henley-on-Thames. *Telephone* Turville Heath 226.

Lying roughly in the same remote area as The Beehive at Russell's Water, The Crown is, perhaps, a shade easier to find. From Nettlebed the road to Watlington runs north, and the second of two right-hand turns brings us on to the lane to Pishill, and eventually to Stonor.

The Crown is so ancient and so picturesque that at first sight one can only stop and stare. Few and far between are inns that look like this. A profusion of wisteria almost covers the front of the building, and the low stone wall at the side leads into a garden of the utmost charm. Across the garden is the old barn, a breath-taking picture of weatherboarding under an enormous thatched roof, with hollyhocks and roses in abundance.

The Crown is said to date from the eleventh century, and no doubt there was a building on the site at that time though no trace now remains. The present inn is mainly Tudor, and the immense beams within bear testimony to this. In such a picturesque building there is no need for added ornaments and the licensee has very wisely refrained from festooning the beams with horse-brasses or cluttering-up the walls with carriage-lamps. An old print mentions that at one time Jesuit priests were in hiding on the premises, and that ghostly murmurings and unaccountable noises have been heard at night.

51

The old barn already mentioned is given over to dancing at week-ends, and The Crown is therefore a most popular place despite its isolated position. Of local trade there is none—there are no locals. But even to those whose dancing days are over it is an attraction in being a free house, with an interesting range of beers, from Morland's bitter to draught Skol.

RADCOT

Swan Hotel

Brewer Morland. *Bedrooms* 6. *Food* Restaurant. *Route* A4095 Faringdon-Witney. *Nearest station* Faringdon. *Telephone* Clarfield 220.

The road from Faringdon to Witney enters Oxfordshire at Radcot, crossing the Thames by way of a hump-back bridge and a series of acute bends. Here the river divides for a short distance, forming an island and a perfect playground for the picnickers, anglers and others who flock to this attractive spot.

The Swan Hotel is on the Oxfordshire bank, and makes the most of its pleasant position. Smooth and well-cared-for lawns run down to the river-bank, a quiet backwater almost encircles the hotel garden, affording private mooring for boats, and the angler may cast his line from the quiet comfort of the stone terrace adjoining. It is, of course, a residential hotel and Morland's supply the beer. Not that you have to fish, or boat or do anything so strenuous if you don't want to.

For many, to sit on the terrace with a pint, watching their fellow-men working up a thirst, is by far the best means of passing the time. And nowhere will it pass more pleasantly than here.

RUSSELL'S WATER

The Beehive

Free House. Food Restaurant. *Special drinks* Worthington E, Draught Guinness, Flowers' Bitter and Keg, Watney's Red Barrel, Draught Cider. *Nearest station* Henley-on-Thames. *Telephone* Nettlebed 306.

The main trouble about The Beehive is that it is almost impossible to find. It lies in the confusing country north of the A423 Henley to Oxford road about three miles from Nettlebed and the same distance west of Stonor. This is a country of wooded valleys and open commonland, the higher points providing endless vistas across the beechwoods, undeniably lovely at all times of the year but at their best in the autumn.

Russell's Water is such a common, with The Beehive beautifully situated in a cluster of buildings grouped round the village pond.

It is certainly a place worth finding. The inn was built in 1610. This is old enough, yet somehow it manages to convey a sense of genuine age not found in many pubs built a hundred years earlier. This is probably due to the intriguing internal lay-out of The Beehive, with odd rooms leading off from the main bars, uneven floors, and furniture at least as old as the pub itself.

The saloon-bar counter is topped with copper, and the base is faced with old sherry barrels cut in two. A massive ingle-nook and old settles contribute to the atmosphere, one of the settles at least dating back to 1620.

It is a free house, providing seven or eight draught beers and for those who need it offers a good selection of pipe-tobacco.

In a pub of this name it is almost inevitable that the conveniences should be labelled 'Queens' and 'Drones'. Some, who have known the place in the past, maintain that even so the distinction is not broad enough!

SANDFORD-ON-THAMES

The King's Arms

Brewer Courage. *Bedrooms* 3. *Food* Snacks. *Special drinks* Draught Guinness. *Route* A423 Oxford–Wallingford. *Nearest station* Oxford. *Telephone* Oxford 77095.

From Magdalen Bridge the Henley road runs south, leaving Oxford by way of Iffley and crossing the southern by-pass two miles from the city centre. A mile farther on a partially concealed finger-post pointing right directs one down a narrow lane towards the river. From this point on there is no possibility of missing The King's Arms, for the lane terminates not only on the river-bank but also in the car-park of this Simonds pub, now part of the Courage group.

It is a popular pub, as most riverside pubs are, and though not particularly old or picturesque the site is a pleasant one. There is a lock not far away, and a little bridge connects with an island and leads eventually to the Berkshire bank.

The King's Arms has two large bars, the saloon being the more attractive of the two with its wood partition and high chairs at the counter. There is draught Guinness, there are snacks, there is pipe-tobacco in quantity. And there is always the river. Small wonder that so many Oxford citizens, setting out on the Henley road, get no farther than the Sandford turn.

SHIPTON-UNDER-WYCHWOOD

The Shaven Crown

Brewer Flowers. *Bedrooms* 14. *Food* Restaurant. *Route* A361 Burford–Chipping Norton. *Nearest station* Shipton. *Telephone* Shipton-under-Wychwood 330.

Five miles north of Burford the road to Chipping Norton, hitherto straight, plunges into a series of sharp bends as it drops down to Shipton and the Evenlode Valley. The village is small, though one of the prettiest on this road, and The Shaven Crown on a bend opposite the village green, makes its own contribution to the beauty of the place.

Built in stone in the fourteenth century by the monks of Bruern Abbey, it certainly looks much more like a monastic building than an inn. Few inns, for instance, can boast a perfect fourteenth-century perpendicular gateway, or a little stone-walled courtyard in which time seems to have lost any meaning. The whole atmosphere is one of great age—and of great peace.

As might be expected this guest-house to the monastery fell a victim to the Dissolution. Unexpectedly, however, it caught the eye of no less a personage than Queen Elizabeth who used it as a shooting-box when hunting in the Forest of Wychwood, which at that time covered the area.

The charm of the building must have had its effect on the Virgin Queen, or she took the unusual course of presenting it to the villagers of Shipton on condition that henceforth it was used as an inn, the landlord paying £20 year to charity in lieu of rent. And an inn it has remained ever since.

Today it is owned by Flowers and remains one of their most interesting nd attractive properties. The visitor to Shipton is just as likely to fall in love vith it today as Queen Elizabeth did five hundred years ago.

SONNING EYE

The French Horn

Free House. Bedrooms 4. Food Restaurant and grill-room. NO DRAUGHT BEER. *Route B478. Nearest station Twyford. Telephone* Sonning 2204.

Though most of Sonning lies on the Berkshire bank of the Thames, part of the parish does extend across the river into Oxfordshire. It is in this part hat The French Horn lies, a large late-Victorian building with gardens loping to the river's brink.

The French Horn is, of course, more an hotel than a pub. But it is an nteresting place, and there is nothing to stop the casual caller from using he bar. This is a most attractive room, with an odd little alcove at each end, one furnished in Victorian style, the other in a more modern idiom. But lthough the casual caller may sup his drink here The French Horn takes no chances on the type of people who might visit it. The absence of draught bitter and the substitution of keg-type ale is an increasingly common feature of the better-class hotel bar today. Here, The French Horn goes one better and sells no draught beer in any form, only bottled. But the array of Scotch and other spirits goes a long way to make up for this, though why a drinker of bottled beer should be considered in a higher social scale than the drinker of draught beer is a little difficult to understand.

The French Horn, it will be seen, is a very plush place. But for all its plushness it is a friendly one. The interior décor is delightful, with wrought-ironwork much in evidence and including a wrought-iron lift!

An attractive feature is the enormous open fireplace in the centre of the lounge-bar. It also includes a spit, complete with hooks and chains, with which ducklings are roasted before the admiring gaze of the genteel

audience. In keeping with the general character of the place, the spit is no
worked by clockwork but by the most silent of electric motors.

The roasting of ducklings is considered to be a *pièce de résistance*, perhap
an unfortunate description as they are, in fact, most tender.

The large windows of the dining-room look out on to the river and th
Berkshire bank, where the picturesque village of Sonning sits in the sun.

It is a delightful spot, and though at first sight The French Horn ma
typify late-Victorian or Edwardian opulence, it is by no means 'stuffy'. Bu
never, never, ask for a pint of mild-and-bitter. The only thing more likel
to increase the barman's blood-pressure would be to dance 'Knees u
Mother Brown' in the lounge.

STANTON HARCOURT

The Harcourt Arms

Brewer Morrell. *Food* Snacks. *Route* B4449. *Nearest station* Eynsham. *Tele
phone* Standlake 322.

Six miles due west of Oxford, Stanton Harcourt lies in the flat fertile plai
between Windrush and Thames. The Harcourts have been lords-of-th
manor since the sixteenth century, though the present Lord Harcourt is th
first of his line to live in the village for over two hundred years.

The Harcourt Arms is a pleasant creeper-covered stone building datin
from about 1720. It was in that year that the manor-house finally becam
uninhabitable through neglect and part of the stones were used in th
building of the inn.

It is unfortunate, in a way, that the interior of The Harcourt Arms doe
not fulfil the promise of the exterior. In the saloon, on the left of the quain
protruding porch, there is a massive fireplace which gives character to th
room. In the recesses of the chimney-piece are various items of brass-war
including, of all things, a splendid brass fireman's helmet. But the rest o
the room seems to try to detract as much as possible from the effect of th
fire-place, and a banal décor of unpleasant wallpaper and a modern woo
overmantle of doubtful taste do all they can to remind one of a dentist'
waiting-room. Still, the licensee manages to overcome these drawbacks, a

all good licensees do. At least the brewers have not put in formica-topped tables—though it is whispered that even this monstrous idea was at one time mooted.

At week-ends, and most evenings during the summer, The Harcourt Arms is busy. One cannot see the wallpaper and nobody worries about the overmantle. Fortunately sanity has prevailed outside. The arms of the Harcourt family displayed on the wall have not been done in coloured plastic.

STEEPLE ASTON

Hopcroft's Holt

Brewer Ind Coope. *Bedrooms* 8. *Food* Restaurant. *Route* A423 Oxford–Banbury. *Nearest station* Bicester. *Telephone* Steeple Aston 254.

The romantic figure of the eighteenth-century highwayman, robbing the coaches and stealing from the passengers with exquisite courtesy, is more a fiction than a fact. Highwaymen there certainly were, but their behaviour was far from genteel and most finished on the gallows to the approving howls of the mob.

Six miles south of Banbury on the Oxford road the Hopcroft's Holt commemorates a highwayman whose name has been associated with elegant behaviour for over two hundred years. This was the Frenchman, Claude Duval, whose association with the innkeeper Hopcroft made this stretch of road notorious in an age when highwaymen were commonplace.

Hopcroft's Holt is today a pleasant pub and quite respectable. The many-gabled stone building stands by the roadside near the village of Steeple Aston attracting notice initially by its beautifully carved sign of the galloping highwayman with the gallows behind him. It is an Ind Coope inn, long and rambling, with a good car-park and plenty of room in the two bars. The 'Farmers Bar' is the public, the 'Heythrop Bar' the cocktail lounge.

It was built in 1734 on the site of a previous inn which Claude Duval must have known well. Relics of this picturesque figure can be seen, including a portrait, and very handsome he was. But his looks and his charm did not save him. Like his other famous associates, Dick Turpin and Jack Sheppard, he finally swung at Tyburn. The gallows on the sign is not there for nothing.

TACKLEY

Sturdy's Castle

Brewer Ind Coope. *Food* Snacks. *Route* A423 Oxford–Banbury. *Nearest station* Bicester. *Telephone* Tackley 209.

The number of people setting themselves up to be experts on inn-signs increases daily. Amiable clerics, lecturers to Women's Institutes and retired military-men profess an intimate knowledge of the subject—but few will know the sign of this inn. The illustration is of two men obviously engaged in a struggle to the death, but this gives little clue to the name. The answer is that the protagonists are named respectively Sturdy and Castle, and this is strictly the correct name of this old posting-house. One killed the other at some time in the eighteenth century, the victor being eventually hanged on the gallows which stood at this spot.

Sturdy's Castle is a plain building of Oxfordshire stone standing on the main Oxford to Banbury road about eight miles out of the city. Neither externally nor internally is there much sign of old age though it has been an inn for well over three hundred years. The outside stone walls show few signs of weathering, and the inside has been completely modernised by the brewers, Messrs. Ind Coope Ltd.

For many years the place was woefully neglected, so much so that when the time came for renovations it was felt that the replacement of beams and other important parts of the fabric would have to be on such an extensive scale that the final effect could only be spurious.

The modernisation was carried out mainly in stone and light wood panelling, and it is most successful. Both lounge and public-bar are bright and cheerful, with that indefinable character which is the hall-mark of a good modernisation, but which is all too rare in old inns.

Behind the scenes some relics of the past still exert their influence. The water is still obtained from the original springs which served the place for centuries. Modern methods of hygiene call for a much greater consumption of water than in the past—and occasionally the wells give out. Maybe, at one time, Sturdy was the landlord and Castle the local plumber—in which case the murder may well have been justified.

TETSWORTH

The Swan

Free House. Bedrooms 22. *Food* Dining-room and grill-room. *Special drinks* Worthington E, Draught Bass, Draught Guinness, Double Diamond, Watney's Red Barrel, Flowers' Keg, Mitchell & Butler. *Route* A40. *Nearest station* Thame. *Telephone* Tetsworth 258.

The unlovely village of Tetsworth lies on the A40 almost exactly half-way between High Wycombe and Oxford. The Swan is about the only picturesque building in the place, but it certainly makes up for the rest. The petrol pumps which abound indicate that Tetsworth is still seeing to the needs of the traveller, as it has been doing since 1362 when The Swan was first mentioned. This rambling brick-built old coaching-inn, with its big courtyard in front, lies right by the main road at the bottom of the hill as you come from High Wycombe. The interior is heavy with black beams, high-backed settles in the bar and that air of being used to coping with cold and weary travellers which is the hall-mark of the good coaching-inn.

The dining-room, though modernised, is in the same idiom, and caters efficiently for the many who make use of this popular pub. The kitchen-

The Swan

59

gardens provide most of the vegetables, and there is a pleasant garden for the residents in addition.

Inns of this age frequently boast with pride that 'Queen Elizabeth slept here'. If this is true of every inn which makes the claim, the Virgin Queen must have spent her entire life in bed—which sounds inconsistent and in any case is untrue. The Swan makes no such claim—but it is a fact that before the young Queen Victoria came to the throne she was at school at Oxford, and occasionally stopped the night at The Swan on her way to London.

This, and the fact that in 1482 the landlord was indicted at Oxford Assizes for overcharging, are the only two claims to fame The Swan makes. And, of course, the fact that it is a free house and supplies at least eight or nine different brews of beer including draught Bass and draught Guinness.

THAME

The Bird-Cage

Brewer Courage. *Bedrooms* 3. *Food* Snacks at all times. *Route* A4129. *Nearest station* Thame. *Telephone* Thame 46.

Originally more than twice the size it is today, The Bird-Cage has been a feature of Thame market-place since 1430. Though the newer buildings near it have tended to compress it they have certainly not overshadowed it and in fact serve to heighten the contrast between the new shop-fronts and the remarkable appearance of this ancient pub.

The great twisted beams of the outside walls, the beautiful oriel windows of the first floor, with its projecting timbers all make The Bird-Cage look more like a fairy-tale drawing than part of a busy market-town.

For centuries the cellars of this place were used as a prison for those transgressing the market regulations, and during the Napoleonic Wars were used as a prisoner-of-war cage for captured French troops. It was during this period that the original name of The Blackbird was changed to include the new function, becoming The Bird-and-Cage, subsequently shortened to The Bird-Cage of today.

Inside, The Bird-Cage is full of interest. There is a large public-bar at the

60

The Bird-Cage

front of the building, with beams of a size rarely seen and confirming the great age of the fabric. There is the base of a huge Elizabethan chimney-stack which goes right up through the upper rooms and seems to take the weight of the entire structure. The smaller saloon-bar at the side has less evidence of age, though here again there is plenty of timber, notably in the ceiling, giving a sense of space and loftiness. Narrow and twisted stairs lead to the upper rooms, each seemingly at a different level, and worlds away from the busy pub below.

Courage's own The Bird-Cage today, and the vast cellars are used for their proper function of storing draught beer. Not that they were entirely wasted even when housing French prisoners, for these industrious soldiers passed part of the time by forming the first Masonic Lodge in Thame.

After several years incarceration in a beer-cellar many would have been more inclined to form a Temperance branch.

THAME

The Black Horse

Brewer Aylesbury Brewery Co. *Bedrooms* 7. *Food* Restaurant. *Special drinks* Ind Coope's Bitter and Mild, Draught Guinness, Watney's Red Barrel. *Route* A4129. *Nearest station* Thame. *Telephone* Thame 286.

The immensely wide high street of this busy market-town includes a surprising number of pubs, varying widely in their appeal and each with characteristics of its own.

From the direction of Princes Risborough, The Black Horse is about half-way along on the left, a neat and attractive-looking pub with a half-timbered frontage. It is an odd sort of shape inside, the saloon heavy with panelling and giving an impression of being smaller than it really is. Leading off this bar is a covered patio, gay with flowers, and a pleasant addition to the interior.

It is becoming more and more common to find pubs selling chocolates, sweets and other peace-offerings for delinquent husbands. The Black Horse is different in that the chocolates on sale are specially made for the house.

The Black Horse may not be typical of Thame pubs, but it has that rare quality, individuality. Even when it is time to go the fateful hour is signalled by the ringing of a Swiss cowbell of stupendous proportions. It is certainly effective, and may be a subtle reminder of the milk chocolate you forgot to buy!

WATLINGTON

The Hare & Hounds

Brewer Morrell. *Food* Snacks at bar. *Route* B4009. *Nearest station* Thame. *Telephone* Watlington 329.

Situated at the foot of the Chilterns three miles south of the London–Oxford main road, Watlington lies red-bricked, snug and asleep. The town centres round the seventeenth-century market-hall, and The Hare & Hounds opposite. It is a Morrell house, old and comfortable, and was at one time the main coaching-inn of Watlington. The saloon-bar, heavy with panelling, and decorated with sporting-prints is certainly more Dickensian in style than Elizabethan, which is the true age of this building.

The large public-bar has a fine old ingle-nook, a collection of wooden spades and other agricultural tools, and more prints. Possibly in an attempt to keep the youth of Watlington off the streets it also has a piano, a television set and a juke-box. Whether or not this laudable ambition succeeds only the authorities can tell. Certainly the bar seems always full—but there are also plenty of young folk in the streets. Perhaps they don't drink, or if they do they may be allergic to television and juke-boxes in pubs. In this they are not alone.

It is probably unfair to describe Watlington as 'decrepit' as one writer has done. It is kinder to call it quiet and forgotten. Forgotten, that is, except for one thing. It was here that the great Buckinghamshire patriot, John Hampden, rested the night before the Battle of Chalgrove Field in which he received his mortal wound, to die at Thame six days later. A small enough claim to fame, perhaps, but the best Watlington can do.

WESTON-ON-THE-GREEN

The Ben Johnson

Brewer Ind Coope. *Food* Restaurant in bar (cold buffet). *Route* A43. *Nearest station* Bicester. *Telephone* Bletchington 230.

Weston-on-the-Green is a pretty, straggling little village of thatched, stone cottages just off the main Brackley to Oxford road (A43) where it joins the Bicester road. The Ben Jonson lies on the main road itself, and like the remainder of the village, is of stone construction with a thatched roof.

It is an Ind Coope house with a reputation for good food. The lounge-bar is a long and attractive room, low and mellow with beams of a dark brown hue which blend admirably with the light Cotswold stone of the walls. At the end of the room, near the fire, one may dine in comfort and gaze at the lesser mortals at the bar, in that superior manner which only

well-fed diners assume. The public-bar is smaller, but has the big stone fir
place of the original inn still intact.

The great stone flags of the cellar, which can be seen from the loung
indicate that originally brewing was done on the premises, and it is pleasa
to catch a glimpse of the oak beer barrels within and to realise that be
'from the wood' is not yet an anachronistic term.

Apart from The Ben Jonson, the delights of Weston are many. Th
church has a most interesting painted altar-piece, and the village stocks a
still to be seen on the green, only a few yards from the pub.

WHEATLEY

The King's Arms

Brewer Ind Coope. *Route* A40. *Nearest station* Oxford. *Telephone* Wheatle
701.

Long ago the village of Wheatley lay on the old road from London t
Oxford five miles away. Came the new A40 trunk road to by-pass th
village, though The King's Arms was fortunately placed at the junction c
the old and new roads.

Today the main road and the whole of the village is by-passed in turn b
a newer trunk road, leaving Wheatley apparently high-and-dry, and acces
sible from the new road only by the negotiation of a bridge and sever
complicated junctions. But no doubt The King's Arms will survive. I
certainly shows no signs of ailing up to now.

It is an old pub and during the reign of George III was used as the loca
magistrates' court. The interior has some fine panelling in the corridors an
in the saloon-bar, and in this bar is displayed the royal coat-of-arms, carve
in wood and painted in its original colours. The small, curved counter i
actually built into the site of the enormous fireplace, giving at the same tim
character and additional space to the room.

Across a beam in the public-bar there is an astonishing collection of fire
marks. Evidently the previous owners were taking no chances, and in th
days when the volunteer fire-brigades worked with their own insuranc
companies, and dealt only with their own fires, the landlord of The King'

Arms was obviously fully covered. These plates were found in the cellars of the inn during alterations, and seem to indicate that the well-known tenacity of the present-day insurance-salesman has roots going back at least two hundred years.

WITNEY

The Marlborough Arms Hotel

Brewer Hunt Edmunds. *Bedrooms* 14. *Food* Restaurant and grill-room. *Route* A415. *Nearest station* Witney. *Telephone* Witney 152.

Few towns have such an air of 'worthiness' and solidity as Witney. The wide main street with shops and inns of weathered stone, the green with its surrounding neat cottages and the seventeenth-century Butter Cross all combine to give an air of homeliness suggesting, as Joanna Cannan remarks, 'a country face scrubbed clean with soap and water'.

The Marlborough Arms, in the middle of the main street, has this same air. It is a good building, with the painted arms of the Dukes of Marlborough on the outside wall and a look of prosperity which avoids self-satisfaction.

It was, of course, an old coaching-inn, and is now an hotel in the Hunt Edmunds group. The extensive modernisation has been carried out with care and with taste, and the appropriately named Blenheim Bar has a most interesting collection of maps and pictures relating to the Duke's campaigns.

Witney's prosperity springs from the development of the wool-mills which commercialised a cottage-industry dating from the time of Edward III. The industry still continues, and Witney blankets are known all over the world. Despite the advent of other industries, such as the manufacture of sausages and pies, Witney remains unspoilt.

The A40 to Cheltenham and Gloucester just touches the northern end of the town, then branches immediately right past one of the mills to continue up-hill to Burford. It is well worthwhile not to turn right, but to go straight on up the main street to the green and explore this charming town for a while.

WITNEY

The Rowing Machine
FETTIPLACE ROAD

Brewer Flowers. *Food* Restaurant and grills. *Special drinks* Big range of wines.
Route South of A40 at Witney. *Nearest station* Witney. *Telephone* Witney
830.

Smith's Estate, on which The Rowing Machine is situated, is a new development on the western side of Witney just south of the A40 main road to
Gloucester. Though it is not far away the little River Windrush has nothing
to do with the name of this pub. Nor does it imply any connection with
aids to physical fitness, except that required to raise a pint tankard from the
counter.

The Rowing Machine

The name, in fact, refers to an old process in the manufacture of blankets, for which Witney is world famous. The rowing-machine was a horse-driven contraption used for raising the pile, in the days when men worked as hard as horses.

This new Flowers pub has been designed to cater not only for the estate, but for the main-road traveller as well. The saloon-bar, with its ship-lap ceiling, venetian blinds and thick carpets is a split-level affair, the higher plane being devoted to food. The walls in this part are decorated with large and interesting photographs illustrating the production of various wines—a subtle encouragement to the diner to discuss this pertinent subject.

Here and there illustrations adorn the walls, many dealing with the history of blanket-making and showing the process alluded to in the name. Though this is indeed a modern pub, there are plenty of reminders of the past to be noted. Perhaps the saddest of these is an old bill of 1782 from the blanket-mill, from which we learn that the man who watched the horse do the work drank a total of 196 pints of beer at a cost to the management of 22s. 8d. But then, watching horses work is a notoriously thirsty pastime—or used to be.

WOODSTOCK

The Bear

Free House. Bedrooms 16. *Food* Restaurant. *Special drinks* Worthington E, Hunt Edmunds' Best Bitter and Gold Top. *Route* A34. *Nearest station* Handborough. *Telephone* Woodstock 511.

To many visitors the little town of Woodstock is merely a preliminary to entering the grounds of Blenheim Palace. This is a pity. Woodstock itself is very worthy of attention and tends to consider the Palace something of an upstart. This attitude is found in many places in the town, and in particular at The Bear in the cobbled market-place, which proudly proclaims 'old when the Palace was new'.

This is certainly true. This dignified stone-fronted coaching-inn can boast a licence as far back as 1232, though the present structure is mainly Tudor. The market-place is just off the High Street and on the way to the main entrance of the Palace. It is surrounded by old buildings, the most notable being the Town Hall, presented to Woodstock by the third Duke of Marlborough and bearing his coat-of-arms. In common with most old coaching-inns the courtyard of The Bear has been covered in. But the archway is still there and leads one into a wide passage where the curious bow-windows of the adjoining rooms remind one vividly that these were originally outside walls looking on to the yard. The main bar is on the right of the arch, a large heavily timbered room with an enormous fireplace. On the left is the more modern but very attractive Games Room.

The Bear is a free house, as most hotels are. And as an hotel it can offer a wine-list longer than most, and a menu more mouth-watering than most.

Winston Churchill was born at Blenheim Palace and is buried in the churchyard at Bladon on the southern edge of the Palace grounds. For this and many other reasons Blenheim attracts thousands of visitors yearly. But

The Bear

Woodstock was there before it, and The Bear, and the Black Prince, and Henry II with his Fair Rosamund and (some say) Geoffrey Chaucer, who is thought to have been born there.

'Old when the Palace was new' applies to a great deal of Woodstock—except the Town Hall.

II

Buckinghamshire

ADSTOCK

The Folly Inn

Free House. Food Snacks at bar. *Special drinks* 'Noggin' Keg, Draught Younger's Bitter. *Route* A413. *Telephone* Winslow 71.

Some two miles north of Winslow, along the Buckingham road, stands The Folly Inn. It seems at first sight to be isolated, but the village of Adstock is not far away just off the main road.

The building itself is unpretentious externally, and although there has been an inn here for many years the present building is probably late-Victorian.

This is another free house in an area where this system seems to thrive. It is also in the area of the Whaddon Chase, and this, no doubt, accounts for the large and interesting hunting mural which is painted above the bar. There is a lounge and a little buttery, both modern in style and both inviting. The bar painting is not the only example of artistic effort in the room, some very fine etchings adorning the walls in addition. But there are at least two more surprises which the visitor to The Folly will discover. The public-bar is situated on the first floor, an unusual enough arrangement. In addition this bar boasts a genuine old-English skittle alley alongside the more familiar darts and bar-billiards.

Those who know only the American ten-pin bowling will quickly discover how difficult is the real art of skittles. Like 'Ringing-the-Bull' and other bar-parlour games of the past it is very difficult to find in present-day pubs. But such games are worth preserving, if only to remind us that our ancestors were quite capable of keeping their wits about them, even when drinking, and played as strenuously as they worked.

AMERSHAM

The Elephant & Castle

Brewer Wethered. *Food* Hot lunches daily (cold buffet Sat./Sun.), cold buffet evenings. *Route* A413. *Nearest station* Amersham. *Telephone* Amersham 410.

The slow curve of Amersham High Street presents a miniature exhibition of architecture of the last five hundred years. It is one of the most attractive streets in the whole of Buckinghamshire, and half-way along on its northern side The Elephant & Castle makes its own contribution to the display.

Though the two gables and half-timbered front have presented the same appearance for many years, internally this pub has had a great deal done to it. This is just as well. At one time the trade was confined to the public-bar, then an uninviting room with an unattractive clientèle. The brewers, Wethered of Marlow, decided to do something about it, and very well they have done it. The public-bar, now called The Elephant Bar, is still there, though much livelier and sprucer than it was. The saloon lounge on the right has also had the 'full treatment' and is, today, a long and pleasant room with many rafters, a workable length of counter and a chimney corner big enough to seat four people if they are on good enough terms.

The beer comes as Barleycorn in the keg, and draught bitter affectionately known locally as 'Tadpole Tested'. This is not the official name, we hasten to add, but springs from the fact that the little River Misbourne, which runs alongside the pub, occasionally seeps into the cellar. But Amersham landlords are used to the behaviour of their rather erratic river, which has been doing this for several hundred years, and nothing is allowed to affect the beer.

There are always snacks to be had at The Elephant, and the lunch-menu is of astonishing variety, the portions being realistic in size and well visible to the naked eye. Two other pleasant features of this pleasant pub should be recorded. The floral decorations are superb, and the landlord smokes a pipe and caters for fellow-addicts.

AMERSHAM

The Griffin

Free House. Food Restaurant and separate snack-bar. *Special drinks* Worthington E, Draught Bass, Flowers' Keg. *Route* A413. *Nearest station* Amersham. *Telephone* Amersham 75.

he old part of Amersham lies on the London to Aylesbury road (A413).
he approach from the London end is hardly picturesque, with its petrol-
ations, and London Transport garage, however necessary they may be.
ist before the traffic-lights marking the junction with the High
Vycombe road (A404) we suddenly realise this really is an old town.
head lies the Market Hall built in 1682, and immediately on the left is The
riffin.

This old three-storeyed inn, with its gables, cobbled archway and court-
ard beyond, has seen a good deal of Amersham history. Religious
ersecution has been a notable feature, from Lollards to Quakers, and
ne local magistrate took it upon himself to rush from The Griffin to
op a Quaker funeral. The coffin was turning the corner on the way
the Friends' Meeting House in the Wycombe road—but he stopped
so effectively that it lay in the road for three days before being laid to
st.

But that was a long time ago. Rarely, these days, is there need to rush from
he Griffin with such haste. The bar is on the left, just under the arch, whilst
n the right is the snack-bar. The former has a comparatively small counter,
it plenty of room to sit in comfort. One can therefore stay and chat at the
ir, but at the same time have every excuse for moving away, should it be
xpedient, to sit in the wonderful high-backed chair which dominates the
om. The sight of the many diners, tottering from the restaurant and
ildly searching for their coats, is always entertaining.

Another present-day link with the past is The Griffin Club. This has been
oing on for two hundred years or more, and is an association of local
usiness people who meet monthly and do good by contributing unobtru-
vely to various local causes. Do not be misled, however, if a pint is bought
r you soon after your arrival. This will not be The Griffin Club, however
eserving you may seem, but merely a symptom of the friendliness The
riffin exhibits to the stranger who drops in.

In addition to its other attractions, The Griffin is a free house, dealing
draught Bass, Flowers' Keg and Worthington E. Apart from the car-park
nder the arch there is an official one just the other side of the road. What
ith that and the traffic-lights it is difficult to see how anybody can avoid
opping for a 'quick one'—unless, of course, a Quaker funeral happens to
e turning the corner!

AMERSHAM

The Nag's Head

Brewer Wethered. *Bedrooms* 3. *Food* Snacks at bar. *Special drinks* Draught Cider. *Route* A404. *Nearest station* Amersham. *Telephone* Amersham 1590.

The A404, running northwards from High Wycombe, finally gets into open country at Hazlemere. From there to Amersham, five miles on, the road runs across what used to be called Wycombe Heath, flat on one side but on the other looking down towards Penn Bottom and its wonderful vista of beeches. The road reaches Amersham via the hospital, and The Nag's Head stands ready and waiting just before the junction with the Aylesbury-London road (A413), on the left.

The rather plain front of this pub is improved by the gay window-boxes looked after with care, and with expert attention. And this is a clue to the character of The Nag's Head. This is in every sense a 'local', and a 'local' that gets its business to a very large extent from the keen gardeners and allotment-holders of the town. The large public-bar and club-room between them contain, at times, more information on the propagation of sweet-peas and the private life of the runner-bean than could be found in the *Encyclopedia Brittanica*. The rear of The Nag's Head includes a small but cosy saloon-bar, where the conversation is less botanical but more personal. A visit to this pub will ensure that you come away knowing either a great deal more about vegetables—or a great deal more about Amersham.

ASTON CLINTON

The Oak

Brewer Aylesbury Brewery Co. *Food* Snacks. *Special drinks* Ind Coope Bitter and Mild, Draught Guinness, Watney's Red Barrel. *Route* Off A41 *Nearest station* Tring.

Practically the whole of the village of Aston Clinton, except the church, lies north of the A41, midway between Aylesbury and Tring. This is the old

Roman Akeman Street, and it is here that the much older Icknield Way crosses the Roman road.

Aston Clinton has stepped aside from the rush of main-road traffic, and The Oak seems even more determined to get as far as possible away from it all. It is almost the last building in the village, and less than a mile from that other important thoroughfare, the Grand Union Canal.

The Oak is old—really old, and it remains very much a little country pub. There is only one public room, and there is no bar. Solid tables and chairs provide the furniture, with wooden stools obligingly left by the Yorkshire Cavalry in 1914. The ceiling is low, and there is an ancient ingle-nook.

With that cheerful disregard for convenience found in most domestic buildings up to Victorian times, the cellar is at the opposite end of the house from the tap-room. Nobody minds, of course, and probably not even the landlord would really welcome such a modern innovation as a bar counter.

But no doubt it will come one day. In the meantime The Oak remains an example of what was once a typical village pub, representing an age fast disappearing. The surprising thing is that despite the journey made to produce each pint, it is on the table in very much less time than it takes in more modern and stream-lined places. The house belongs to the Aylesbury Brewery Company, and the beer is Ind Coope's.

AYLESBURY

The Bull's Head

Free House. Bedrooms 32. *Food* Restaurant. *Special drinks* Draught Guinness, Draught Bass, Ind Coope's Bitter. *Nearest station* Aylesbury. *Telephone* Aylesbury 4761.

For nearly five hundred years The Bull's Head has looked out on to the market-place of Aylesbury. It stands on the north side of the square, not far from where the statues of John Hampden and Disraeli helpfully point the way to Amersham and Tring.

Like many other coaching-inns the yard has been covered-in, but the galleries above are still to be seen. It now forms a very comfortable lounge, and in the wall is preserved a section of the original wattle-and-daub construction of 1478. Sporting-prints decorate the walls and there is also an

The Bull's Head

interesting 'Act of Parliament' clock of 1720 a legal requirement for inns in those days for the benefit of those without watches.

Being an hotel The Bull serves good food at all times, and the oak-timbered dining-room has a mellow charm conducive to good digestion.

The two bars, lounge and cocktail, serve a rather unusual combination of beer. There is draught Guinness, draught Bass and Ind Coope's bitter, a beer rarely seen in these parts and well worth sampling when found.

AYLESBURY

The Derby Arms

Brewer Courage. *Food* Snacks at bar. *Nearest station* Aylesbury. *Telephone* Aylesbury 2164.

he oldest and most picturesque parts of a town are usually centred round
e parish church. Aylesbury keeps this tradition, and the narrow passages,
d houses and quiet squares round the churchyard seem totally uncon-
cted with the busy shops and bustling market-place only a stone's-throw
vay.

The Derby Arms is in a narrow lane next to the church. It is an unusual-
oking pub with a prim and dignified front looking on to the churchyard.
was built as a private house early in the seventeen-hundreds and is there-
re less picturesque, in a way, than old pubs usually are. But it is not with-
it interest. The red-brick Georgian front has the symmetry expected of
at era of building, and the front door, with its big portico and Ionic
lasters supporting is a very handsome affair. The front has been extended
wards higher than the building itself, and this gives a slightly theatrical

he Derby Arms

effect when seen from the side. It seems almost as if the façade has bee
superimposed on an existing and much lower building, and the genera
effect is out of the ordinary.

The Derby Arms is a Courage house. Internally it has been modernise
and made into a bright and cheerful series of rooms, leaving nothing visibl
of the original building. But there is a well on the premises—and rumou
of a subterranean passage connecting the house with the church. Even if th
pub has little antiquity within it is the sort of place in which the imaginatio
can wander—and a good centre from which to explore Aylesbury.

AYLESBURY

The Duck   BEDGROVE ESTAT

Brewer Courage. Food Snacks at bar. Route A41. Nearest station Aylesbury
Telephone Aylesbury 4878.

It is a characteristic of English main roads that in open country they ar
often narrow and twisting, becoming straight and wide only at the begin
ning of a built-up area with the corresponding imposition of a speed-limi
The A41 London to Birmingham road is no exception to this, and it is o
the London side of Aylesbury that this tortuous road suddenly become
bearable just as it reaches the first housing estates of the town. This is wher
we find The Duck, a modern pub almost as new as the Bedgrove Estat
which it serves.

It is a long and flat-topped building, functional in design and obviousl
intended to deal with its thirsty customers with speed and efficiency. Ther
is, of course, a spacious car-park and the main external feature of The Duc
is the attractive veranda almost surrounding it. Internally it is roomy, wit
such modern features as multi-coloured walls and a ceiling of teak timber
The building is divided into two bars, side by side, with a counter runnin
the entire length, an arrangement which tends to negate that indefinabl
pub atmosphere which most customers hanker after. One feels tha
Courage, who own it, may have realised this a little too late and in a
attempt to give it 'cosiness' have adopted the odd expedient of keeping th
bar-counter in semi-gloom whilst the room itself is brightly lit. Unfor
tunately it hasn't come off.

Still, The Duck is an interesting pub for the student of hostelries, and does not have to worry about passing trade. Its customers all know each other and this, after all, is the main reason why people go to pubs. But it could have been done better, and has been in other parts of the county.

AYLESBURY

The King's Head

Brewer Charrington. *Bedrooms* 11. *Food* Restaurant. *Special drinks* Worthington E. *Route* A41. *Nearest station* Aylesbury. *Telephone* Aylesbury 5158.

Aylesbury is rich in old buildings, quiet squares and narrow streets, despite the roar of traffic through the town and the newer developments on the outskirts. But gradually 'progress' is destroying the old buildings, or at least hiding them from view. This has happened to The King's Head, one of the most interesting buildings in the town. So interesting, in fact, that it is now owned by the National Trust, whilst still continuing as an hotel.

It is hidden away behind a modern block, just where Bourbon Street comes into the Market Place. It was built about 1450 as a monastery Guest House, and Henry VIII stayed in it on several occasions before his marriage to Anne Boleyn. On the Dissolution of the Monasteries the house was given to the Earl of Wiltshire, who made it into an inn and took Henry's name as the sign.

From the market-square the archway into the courtyard can be seen. A door on the left leads into the lounge, a comparatively lofty room with blackened oaken posts from which the beams spring. The chief glory of this room, and of the inn, is the wonderful Tudor window with oak mullions, leaded panes and some of the original stained glass still in position. The latter includes the arms of Henry VI and Margaret of Anjou probably inserted after their marriage in 1445 during the construction of the inn.

This window, of course, once looked directly on to the market-square. Now it can be seen only from inside the room, or from the narrow lane outside formed by the new building in front.

Oliver Cromwell made the inn his headquarters during the Civil War, when his troops were stationed in the town. In the seventeenth century The King's Head issued its own coins for a time, and some of these may be seen in the County Museum near by.

Within the archway, beautifully timbered, a twisting seventeenth-century stairway leads to the rooms above. On the right of the courtyard, opposite the old building, a more modern construction replaces the old stables, and provides garages with a useful room for functions and meetings above.

Food is always available, as befits such an ancient inn. It is one of the few houses in this area supplied by Charrington, and their Toby ale is available as keg beer, the I.P.A. as draught. Worthington E is also sold.

BEACONSFIELD

The Earl of Beaconsfield

Brewer Ind Coope. *Food* Restaurant—Specialises in marine food. *Special drinks* Benskin's Bitter. *Route* B474. *Nearest station* Beaconsfield. *Telephone* Beaconsfield 525.

This imposing Victorian building stands just by the railway bridge in the new part of the town, and is more interesting internally than one might think. It has a large public-bar, an enormous saloon-bar, restaurant and annexe for private parties. The décor is modern and includes some charming oil-paintings by the landlord and his wife. In the restaurant they have done a large mural which in itself is quite an eye-opener apart from the unusual ornamentation of bamboo frames surrounding the tables.

The real surprise about this house is that it could well be a place of literary and religious pilgrimage. The annexe was at one time a separate building, and was erected as a private chapel at the turn of the century by a devout Irish Catholic landlord. G. K. Chesterton, who lived at near-by Gerrards Cross, frequently attended services and in fact was received into the Catholic Church in that very room.

On a more material plane The Earl of Beaconsfield is a very good place at which to eat, and oysters are a speciality. The beer is Ind Coope's.

BEACONSFIELD

The Greyhound

Brewer Courage. *Food* Snacks, hot-dogs, etc. *Nearest station* Beaconsfield. *Telephone* Beaconsfield 8473.

The wide and attractive High Street of Beaconsfield is well known to motorists on the London–Oxford road (A40). If you have time it is a good idea to stop and explore. One of the places you will no doubt discover is The Greyhound, a little way down Windsor End at the cross-roads by the church.

Since the fourteenth century The 'Greyhound Dog' (as it was once called) has been providing refreshment for the traveller, though the present building is mainly seventeenth century. The old beams and low ceiling give it a mellow charm, as do the various kitchen utensils decorating the walls. At one time part of the building was used as the village pound, and the old Beaconsfield Brewery stood immediately behind it. A large and pleasant

The Greyhound

upstairs room is the meeting-place of many local associations, and at one time this room was the scene of the annual village dance on Beaconsfield Fair night.

Parking is easy—under the trees on the other side of the road, another reason why The Greyhound is as popular with travellers as with the locals.

BLEDLOW

The Red Lions

Free House. Bedrooms 6. Food Restaurant. *Special drinks* Benskin's Bitter and Mild, Worthington E, Flowers' Bitter, Watney's Red Barrel. *Nearest station* Princes Risborough. *Telephone* Princes Risborough 345.

At the western edge of the village of West Wycombe the road to Bledlow Ridge branches off the A40 and, after running almost under the hill with its famous caves and church, soon begins its climb into the Chilterns.

For two miles it runs along the top of the ridge, affording wonderful views of typical Chiltern scenery and eventually reaching the straggling

The Red Lions

village of Bledlow Ridge. Soon after the village a branch road to the right starts on the downward journey to Bledlow village, and a left turn brings us to The Red Lions.

It is at the end of the village, on rising ground, and is probably one of the most beautifully sited inns for many miles. In front the ground drops away to the Aylesbury plain, while to the south Bledlow Ridge and Wain Hill, with its mysterious cross cut in the chalk, seem to stand guard.

It is a peaceful village, Bledlow. The old houses and church are grouped together in perfect harmony, the church built on a rock above a rushing stream. But The Red Lions, set a little apart from the other buildings, seems more peaceful and relaxed than any of them.

It is a seventeenth-century inn, long and low, and was originally three shepherds' cottages. The massive, square-cut beams emphasise the solid construction of those days, and the varied levels of floor underline the several alterations made during the life of the building. There is a massive fireplace and ingle-nook, and a delightful window-seat giving extensive views across the hills.

The Red Lions is a free house supplying Benskin's, Flowers' and Worthington beers. There is plenty of food including real haggis imported from Scotland weekly.

It is certainly an unusual pub, and even the name is singular in that it is plural.

BLETCHLEY

The Shoulder of Mutton

Brewer Flowers. *Food* Snacks at bar. NO DRAUGHT BEER. *Route* B4034. *Nearest station* Bletchley. *Telephone* Bletchley 3460.

This is a modern house built on the site of a Victorian pub, and serves the newer part of Bletchley on the Buckingham road. It is bright and cheerful, as most modern pubs are, and everywhere is organised for the convenience of the customer. The beer is Flowers, and it is all from the keg—there is no draught. For the older bitter-drinker, set in his ways and notoriously critical of his beer, this might, perhaps, be considered a drawback. But this is the tendency today, and the generation now beginning to develop a palate for beer will one day describe to their grandchildren those far-off days when the beer came in wooden casks, and needed such care before it was ready to sell.

As well as the saloon- and public-bars, The Shoulder of Mutton has a room furnished with diminutive tables and chairs in which the kids can be parked safely whilst bloating themselves with soft drinks.

This is an innovation which might well be copied more often, and no doubt the once-familiar sight of small children playing around the pub doorway will be just as much a memory as the barrels of beer going down the chute.

The Shoulder of Mutton is certainly modern, but there is no lack of character. The tables and chairs on the forecourt speak hopefully of fine weather—and provide an extensive view of the passing traffic.

Inside the bar there is a photograph of the old pub. Even the most hide-bound Victorian, or conservative drinker of bitter, must admit that there has been a vast improvement.

BOOKER

The Turnpike

Brewer Courage. *Food* Snacks at bar. *Route* A404. *Nearest station* High Wycombe. *Telephone* High Wycombe 5519.

This is definitely not a village inn—but a pub built for a purpose. And what better purpose could it have than to slake the thirsts of the residents of the big estates at Booker and Cressex, suburbs of High Wycombe at the top of Marlow Hill.

It stands a few yards down a road to the right of the Wycombe–Lane End road (A404), almost surrounded by an enormous car-park which, despite its size, is nearly always full.

When this pub was built a few years ago the brewers (Courage) decided to call it The Jolly Sandboy. There was an immediate howl of rage from the locals at this, although why such exception was taken is not quite clear.

86

The brewers wisely decided to let the customers name it, and ran a competition, as brewers do in situations like this. The Turnpike was the answer, and indeed there was a turnpike near the spot on the Marlow road long ago. To underline the connection the lounge-bar was promptly given the rather nice name of The Toll-Bar—the public-bar was left to its own devices.

It is a large pub, the Toll-Bar seeming to be the size of the Albert Hall and the public approximating to St Pancras Station. This, however, is an optical illusion, particularly if one has spent a great deal of time visiting low-beamed and cramped village inns of Elizabethan vintage. Here everything is bright and roomy. The service is slick, the decorations attractive, and if you don't want to stand the chairs are extraordinarily comfortable. Happy residents of Booker and Cressex!

BOURNE END

The Firefly

Brewer Benskin. *Bedrooms* 4. *Food* Restaurant. *Route* A4155 Marlow–Bourne End. *Nearest station* Bourne End. *Telephone* Bourne End 97.

The external appearance of this Benskin pub is not in any way glamorous. It was originally called The Railway Hotel—and it looks it. True, a car-park has been added, but the building remains a good example of solid and unimaginative Victorian design, and little can alter it.

Inside, though, it is very different. The brewers spent a great deal of money on this place, and the result is most effective. There is a well-designed saloon lounge with carefully subdued lighting, and a small annexe round the corner where couples can enjoy each others' company and remain practically invisible.

But for those who have passed that soul-searing stage the bar exhibits a wonderful range of drinks, and an equally impressive display of food. There is plenty of room at the handsome, copper-topped counter, and it is the easiest thing in the world to slip away for a couple of minutes to see how the lovers round the corner are getting on. Your drink will still be there when you get back.

There is also a large public-bar adjoining, and a restaurant completes the picture.

Bourne End is a riverside village and therefore much pre-occupied with sailing. It was only natural, therefore, that when Benskin's were looking for a new name for The Railway Hotel in 1956 they chose The Firefly, this being a class of yacht very popular on the river at that time. That particular yacht may have lost its popularity now, but this Firefly looks set for a very healthy future. Particularly if romance continues to blossom in the tactful shade of the saloon-bar annexe.

BOURNE END

The Heart-in-Hand CORES END

Brewer Wethered. *Food* Snacks at bar. *Route* A4094 Maidenhead–High Wycombe. *Nearest station* Bourne End. *Telephone* Bourne End 887.

The eighteenth-century 'marriage-monger', performing his function of doubtful validity, usually worked from licensed premises. A sign such as 'The Heart-in-Hand' or 'The Cross-Hands' was considered to give a feeling of respectability, and though the marriage-mongers are no more, the sign remains.

Here, near the river at Bourne End, The Heart-in-Hand gets its sign from an ancient beer-house near by, where marriage ceremonies were once performed. Today, your matrimonial state will not be queried in this four hundred-year-old pub. Rather will you be invited to look around at the various samples of furnishing and decoration which add so much character to the comfortable lounge. Not that this room is in any sense a museum— everything in it has a purpose. The massive cuckoo-clock regularly reminds one of the approach of 'Time'. The cane-backed armchair is typical of a more Spartan age. In a corner, by the massive fireplace, a delightful Victorian chaise-longue invites one to recline gracefully, to study, at the same time, the disgraceful goings-on in Hogarth's 'Gin Lane' hanging just above. On the wall there is an attractive set of Thomas Shepherd's etchings of 1828 depicting various properties owned by the Licensed Victuallers' Association

It says a great deal for the licensed trade that as long as one hundred and fifty years ago they already had their own almshouses and their own L.V.A. School. The lounge was extended some years ago by the acquisition of a cottage next-door. The ceiling of this building was removed, together with the dividing wall, resulting in half the bar being low whilst the other half goes straight up to the roof. The old timbers of the cottage are plainly visible, and give this large room an atmosphere quite distinct from most other old inns.

Wethered, who are the brewers concerned, must be congratulated on having performed a most effective 'wedding' here, and one likely to last a very long time.

BRADENHAM

The Red Lion

Brewer Wethered. *Food* Snacks at bar. Good lunches. *Route* A4010. *Nearest station* High Wycombe. *Telephone* Naphill 2212.

The road from Walters Ash winds down through the colourful beech-woods, past Bradenham Church and Manor, suddenly erupting on to the main road from West Wycombe to Princes Risborough (A4010). The Red Lion marks the junction of the two roads, though retiring slightly towards the village as if to remind one of its ancient connections.

White walls, green benches and little garden outside make it easy to find as you come along the main road. The two bars inside are snug and cosy, and connected by a curious little passage where, needless to say, someone is always standing.

The Red Lion is a popular stopping-place for food and drink for travellers on this road. It is a Wethered pub, and supplies good but inexpensive lunches. At one time Bradenham was famous for its hams, cured in the village and known through several counties. Though there is nothing to remind us of this former glory, there still remains Bradenham Manor, boyhood home of Benjamin Disraeli, whose father was described by a contemporary as 'the most lovable, perfect old gentleman I ever met with'.

Benjamin sleeps in the churchyard at Hughenden, two miles away, but his father's ghost could still haunt The Red Lion, when some of the locals drop in.

BRILL

The Sun Hotel

Brewer Aylesbury Brewery Co. *Food* Snack-bar in lounge. *Special drinks* Ind Coope's Bitter and Mild, Draught Guinness, Watney's Red Barrel. *Nearest station* Bicester. *Telephone* Brill 208.

To visit Brill at any time is a pleasure, but on a fine day it is an unforgettable experience. Perched 700 feet up on a hill, its famous old mill looking out over the rolling countryside towards Oxford, Brill seems uncannily like a hill-top village of Provence.

The Sun Hotel stands in the main street, at the junction with a lane leading to the mill. It is reputed to be on the site of a coachyard used by Henry VIII when hunting in these parts, and this may well be so. Today it is a rambling building, with unexpected passages and out-houses, and a pleasant, mellow lounge where the hunting motif is used on the walls.

No doubt, in its long history, The Sun has always provided good food. The range of delicacies displayed in the little snack-bar is astonishing, and would put many a larger inn to shame. Unusual also is the fact that The Sun really does cater for the pipe-smoker, and no less than fourteen different brands of tobacco are available.

In mid-Victorian times there was a movement to turn Brill into a fashionable hydro by virtue of the chalybeate spring in the valley below. A pump-house and bath were constructed, but nothing came of the project. Today the buildings lie derelict and crumbling on the hill-side overlooking the plain. Queen Victoria, it seems, was the cause of the trouble, preferring the more sophisticated delights of Leamington Spa which opened about the same time.

Perhaps it is just as well. Those who love the Buckinghamshire country-side would not exchange the charm of this lovely place for all the tea in China—or all the sulphur in the spring. And think what the Victorians might have done with the mill!

BUCKINGHAM

The White Hart

Free House. Bedrooms 19. *Food* Restaurant. *Special drinks* Whitbread's Bitter, Worthington E, Flowers' Keg. *Route* A41. *Nearest station* Buckingham. *Telephone* Buckingham 2131.

The disastrous fire of 1725 destroyed 130 buildings in Buckingham, leaving desolation from which the town has never really recovered. The White Hart, at one time the main posting-inn of the town, escaped the conflagration and still stands today, a worthy member of the Trust Houses group.

The front is Georgian, hiding the real antiquity of the inn with its pine-panelled rooms and deep window-seats. Even more improvements have been made to the interior of The White Hart in latter years, one of doubtful virtue being the creation of a small and characterless bar in the front of the house. However, it is the company one meets that matters, and this bar is popular with local businessmen and farmers and the conversation is entertaining.

The immense kitchen-gardens of this inn include the famous asparagus-beds, and it is from this area, at the back of the building, that the real age of The White Hart can be discerned and the shape of the old building traced.

The White Hart has long been associated with Stowe, two miles away, when it was the seat of the Dukes of Buckingham and more recently since it became a famous public-school. Here again, as at Hartwell, near Ayles-bury, we find a connection with France, for the exiled Comte de Paris, grandson of Louis-Phillipe, died there in 1894. The last Duke of Buckingham had died five years previously, in 1889. It was a short-lived title, created only in 1822, but is at least perpetuated in The White Hart by the many-quartered arms which hang in the dining-room.

91

BURNHAM

The Old Five Bells

Brewer Wethered. *Food* Snacks at bar. *Nearest station* Slough. *Telephone* Burnham 276.

The village of Burnham seems to lead a placid existence, untouched by events and brooding quietly on former glories. It is west of Slough by two miles, and about the same distance north of the bustling A4 Bath road. Once the main road to the west of England went through the village, and stood at an important cross-roads. Now the main road passes it to the south and this road, in turn, is now by-passed by the M4 Motorway.

The quietest place in this quiet village is Church Close. This is a little cul-de-sac off the High Street, the great flint Parish Church on one side, The Old Five Bells on the other.

Burnham is a great centre for bell-ringers in South Buckinghamshire, and it is fitting that an inn of this name should be hard by—for ringing is thirsty work. Not only are the bells shown on the inn-sign, but less usual, two sets of five bells adorn the outside walls.

Within, this Wethered house shows the usual signs of great age, with careful restoration giving added comfort and a sense of space. The L-shaped lounge is attractive, divided in two by a handsome wrought-iron arch resting on low wooden walls. The warm red curtains and furnishings blend admirably with the dark oak and shining brass, and only the expert could tell which is the old and which the new.

The Old Five Bells was at one time the headquarters of the Burnham Volunteer Fire-Brigade. During renovations two fine brass hose-ends were discovered, which now take their rightful place on view in the bar. The regulars comment on this, but Burnham residents are noted for being out-spoken. However, it is unlikely that they will carve their remarks on the ancient woodwork of The Old Five Bells, as a native did in the church two hundred years ago.

'The Pope is a Knave,' he inscribed with feeling on one of the pillars in the south aisle. It is pleasant to think that this spokesman for the Established Church then refreshed himself at the pub opposite. At any rate he returned later and continued his *magnum opus* on the same pillar, but with less accuracy, with the words 'The Pope is a Vilin'. He must have had quite a celebration after that!

CADMORE END

The Blue Flag

Free House. Food Snacks at bar. *Special drinks* Draught Guinness, Younger's 'Tartan', Fremlin's Bitter, Whitbread's Tankard, Draught Bass. *Nearest station* High Wycombe. *Telephone* Lane End 365.

The eight miles of road between Stokenchurch and Marlow is one of the most pleasant stretches in the south of the county. Starting nearly 700 feet up in the Chilterns the road runs through open country most of the way dropping gently down as it nears the Thames at Marlow. Three miles out of Stokenchurch The Blue Flag stands by the roadside marking the presence of the tiny hamlet of Cadmore End.

It is an old inn, long and low, with that air of venerable antiquity coupled with modern comfort which is typical of village inns in these parts. The Chiltern Hills attract the tourists, and the village inns of the district make

The Blue Flag

93

the most of it. Even if some of the timbers are not quite as old as they look, and some of the horse-brasses slightly suspect, who cares? Most of these old pubs are today very much more pleasing to the eye and more comfortable inside than when they were in their original state. Certainly The Blue Flag is a very good example of how an old inn can be improved without losing character. The L-shaped lounge, low and comfortable, is pleasantly adorned with Dickens prints and good brasses. The old beams and timbers are impressive, and mostly the originals. Understandably, in a remote area such as this, The Blue Flag draws its customers from the surrounding district from Lane End and High Wycombe, and from the little villages of Skirmett, Frieth and Turville. The area around is a 'much-favoured one' as the estate-agents say, and notabilities are fairly thick on the ground. Raymond Glendenning and Cassandra both use The Blue Flag at times—and both appreciate a good pub.

CADSDEN, near Princes Risborough

The Plough

Brewer Benskin. *Food* Snacks—cheeses a speciality. *Route* 1 mile off A4010. *Nearest station* Princes Risborough. *Telephone* Princes Risborough 2879.

The ancient Icknield Way, running along the edge of the Chilterns where they drop suddenly to the Vale of Aylesbury, is now the main road from Princes Risborough to Wendover. Some two miles from Princes Ris-borough, along this road, is the Askett cross-roads. A right turn here brings you under the imposing Whiteleaf Hill, with Whiteleaf Cross cut in the turf. The road begins to climb into the hills immediately, but after a mile or so, at the beginning of Longdown Hill, a short track branches to the right, stopping short immediately outside The Plough. This is a very intelligent thing to do, as there is really little point in journeying farther.

The Plough is a delightful place, almost hidden in this little fold of the Chilterns, surrounded by woods and with no other habitation in sight. The old inn has three comfortable bars, Benskin's beer, a sprinkling of old map (not unusual) and some straw dollies (most unusual). There is also plenty of food, which includes thirty varieties of cheese.

The Plough has a long connection with food. On August Sunday is held
the ancient Cherry Pie Feast, at which enormous quantities of this favourite
Buckinghamshire delicacy are doled out. The feast dates back many centuries and is said to commemorate the final picking each year of the famous
'Bucks Black' cherries. There is plenty of room to park, plenty of seats to sit
. outside, and the whole range of the Chiltern woodlands for the kids to get
lost in. What more can thirsty parents require?

CHALFONT ST GILES

The Pheasant

Brewer Benskin. *Food* Restaurant. Snacks at bar. *Route* A413. *Nearest station*
Chalfont and Latimer. *Telephone* Chalfont St Giles 2113.

Much of the charm of Chalfont St Giles centres round the pond and the
lovely little village green. The village is just off the main road, on the way to
Jordans and Seer Green. On this road, but still in Chalfont, is the cottage
owned by John Milton, who came here to escape the Plague and wrote
Paradise Lost in the house.

Up on the London road, with its hurrying traffic, The Pheasant stands at
the cross-roads and manages to get the best of both worlds. It is an interesting
building, set down well below road-level and with a good car-park
adjoining.

In common with many pubs in this part of Buckinghamshire it is owned
by Benskin, the Watford brewers, though they, of course, are now part of
a much larger group. The interior of The Pheasant is unusual. It consists
almost entirely of one long bar, heavily timbered, with a little annexe at one
end to provide seating. Many bars as long as this would lack character and
require the services of a carrier-pigeon to communicate with a person at the
other end. But this bar, in some magical way, avoids this difficulty and one
feels at home in it immediately, and anything but lost. This may be due to
the fact that the beams are decorated with very clever colour sketches of
various customers, done by the licensee in what he laughingly calls his
'spare-time'. Yet another pictorial addition is a broadsheet of about 1830
describing in doggerel verse (as was the fashion of the day) a great scandal

in the district. This was no less than the murder, by a former licensee, of
local farmer who had been causing trouble. These days N.F.U. membe
need have no fear, though the landlord may well execute them in oils. Th
Pheasant is a pleasant pub, and Chalfont St Giles a most charming villag
Why it should have inspired Milton to write *Paradise Lost* has always bee
a great mystery.

CHALFONT ST PETER

The Greyhound

Brewer Harman. *Bedrooms* 8. *Food* Restaurant and snacks at the bar. *Rou*
A413. *Nearest station* Gerrards Cross. *Telephone* Gerrards Cross 3404.

The A40 Trunk road to Oxford and South Wales roars out of London b
way of Acton, Western Avenue and Denham. With understandable reli
the motorist turns off, just past Denham, and picks up the A413 to Ame
sham and Aylesbury.

Immediately, the Chilterns begin. The transformation is spectacular ar
when, after a couple of miles, Chalfont St Peter and The Greyhound a
sighted, you are really in the country.

The Greyhound, in the centre of the village and next to the church, is on
of the best-known coaching-inns in the county. To press the point home
has one of the last stage-coaches to run on this road carefully preserved
the yard.

The old inn has had the original archway closed in and converted into
snug cocktail bar, whilst the side immediately adjoining the main road ha
been demolished, leaving a picturesque L-shaped building set back from th
road. There is a cosy lounge, with high-backed settles and low tables;
larger saloon-bar and a public-bar, all of venerable antiquity, and a fin
collection of old firearms adorns the walls.

An equally fine collection of locals adorns the bars, the public in pa
ticular, whilst the lounge- and cocktail-bars support a good selection
tired businessmen, together with a sprinkling of air-line pilots living ou
of earshot of London Airport.

The beer is Harman's of Uxbridge, and is available as mild, bitter ar
Best Bitter on draught, with Pankard from the keg. Pipe-tobacco is alwa

The Greyhound

in stock, snacks are available at all hours, and lunches and dinners at the usual times every day except Mondays.

In all this is a most comfortable and pleasant inn, and was even considered so by Judge Jeffries, notoriously difficult to please! The room he occupied may be seen.

There is no ghost on the premises but—a word of warning! If, on your way back to London, just before re-joining the A40, you meet a coach-and-four coming at you head-on, don't panic! Don't even think that that last whisky was a mistake! It is a *real* ghost coach you are seeing, and you are indeed honoured. At least, that's what the locals say! No timetables are available!

CHALFONT ST PETER

The White Hart

Brewer Benskin. *Food* Dining-room. *Route* A413. *Nearest station* Gerrards Cross. *Telephone* Chalfont St Giles 2441.

There is really not very much of old Chalfont St Peter still standing. Fortunately, what there is includes the fourteenth-century White Hart just on the left as you come into the village from London.

A public car-park has thoughtfully been provided opposite, but speed is essential when crossing the road to seek sanctuary at the inn. Once inside you have no doubt at all that this is a very old building indeed. Beams, black with age, and massive pillars abound, the floor is uneven and the ceilings low. Nobody over six feet can stand upright without having his head wedged between the rafters, a useful excuse for getting home late. The one bar is small, with an open basket-fire crackling a welcome in winter, ingle-nook and a selection of interesting brassware. Two small but cosy rooms adjoin where one may eat in comfort not a biscuit's toss from the main source of supply.

Ind Coope provide the beer, by way of Best Bitter and Mild drawn from the wood. There is also Watney's Red Barrel in keg. Apart from the more obvious attractions of The White Hart it has two further claims to distinction. It is the headquarters of the Chalfont St Peter Doghouse Club, formed from customers habitually 'in the doghouse' at home and dedicated to the raising of money for charity. Members thus have a perfect excuse for spending the entire evening at The White Hart.

The other attraction is a ghost in the shape (if that is the right word) of a spectral violinist, whose music has been heard in the bar during the silent watches of the night. An eccentric landlord of a century ago was reputed to play his fiddle in the room, completely ignoring his customers' agonised cries for beer. Those who have been privileged to hear him have complained that though he may be in the right bar he is certainly not in the right key!

CHESHAM

The Black Horse   THE VALE

Brewer Benskin. *Food* Snacks and lunches. *Route* Off A416. *Nearest station* Chesham. *Telephone* Chesham 4656.

Chesham, though not itself a very elegant town, has the good fortune to be surrounded by some of the most varied scenery in Buckinghamshire. The

98

The Black Horse

main road through the town is the A416 to Berkhamstead, running along the Chess Valley and then suddenly turning right to climb the slopes to Ashley Green and the county boundary.

The Vale, as its name implies, is the continuation of this valley north of the town. The winding road soon leaves the houses behind and a mile or so on The Black Horse suddenly appears round a bend. It is in a beautiful situation, standing alone by the road, the green slopes behind framing its white walls and ancient timbers. There is a good garden, with trim lawns and rustic furniture, where one may drink in perfect peace and comfort.

Not that The Black Horse isn't comfortable inside, as well. But what catches the eye are the entertaining theatre posters of yesteryear and the Toulouse-Lautrec reproductions which are the main feature.

The beer is Benskin's, and wine is sold by the glass. For more solid fare there are home-made pies and what is called a 'ploughman's lunch' of bread and cheese. But whether you come on foot, by car, or on a tractor, The Black Horse will welcome you as it has welcomed travellers for the past four hundred years.

99

CHESHAM

The George

Brewer Ind Coope. *Bedrooms* 5. *Food* Restaurant. *Special drinks* Benskin's Mild and Bitter. *Route* A416. *Nearest station* Chesham. *Telephone* Chesham 3123.

Very little of old Chesham is still visible in the High Street. Mostly the façade is one of new shop-fronts with only here and there a reminder of the town's age. The George, however, with its swinging sign, can take us back over three hundred years, to the time of the eccentric Roger Crab who opened a hat shop in 1651 and is thought to have been the original of Lewis Carroll's 'Mad Hatter'. Inside it is snug and comfortable, and usually very busy. It is a great meeting-place for the young of Chesham, and various organisations make use of the large room upstairs for gatherings.

The front part of the saloon (there is no public-bar) extends the width of the building. The main part of the bar counter itself forms one side of a

The George

narrow passage leading to the back door. Human nature being what it is, most customers seem to prefer to have their drink standing in the narrowest part, rather than to sit in comfort elsewhere. The old woodwork gives a pleasant and mellow atmosphere whatever part of the pub you happen to be in, and it is not a place one leaves easily. The beer, in common with most Chesham pubs, is Ind Coope's, and a very good lunch may be had.

CHESHAM

The White Horse

Brewer Ind Coope. *Food* Snacks. *Special drinks* Watney's Red Barrel, Benskin's Bitter and Mild. *Route* A416. *Nearest station* Chesham. *Telephone* Chesham 2393.

Although The White Horse is on the main road to Amersham from Chesham it somehow manages to get overlooked by many who must pass it every day. This is probably because it is on an awkward bend just before the hill leading to Amersham, a bend which requires the maximum concentration to negotiate and prohibits any idle glancing around at the scenery. The owners, Messrs. Ind Coope, have therefore avoided any large expenditure on modernisation, and the pub still has the pattern formerly found in nearly all beer-houses in this area. There is a centre passage with a tiny serving-counter, with just one room on each side of it. Obviously this is a pub to sit in rather than to stand around in elegant positions, and the licensee has made it worth sitting in, and has used a great deal of imagination in the process.

A wall of one of the rooms, for instance, is papered entirely with pages from *The Times*—Educational Supplements and all! In addition to this unusual motif, there is a wonderful collection of oil-lamps scattered around the room, and a most fascinating old clock dominating the scene.

So often the only idea a licensee has when he wants to make his pub attractive is to festoon it with fairy-lights. It is a pleasant change to find a place where unusual ideas have been used inside to interest the customer. Maybe one day, if the collection of lamps increases, quite a story might be built up about the origin of it. And the brewers might even consider changing the name from The White Horse to The Foolish Virgin.

COLNBROOK

The Ostrich

Brewer Courage. *Food* Steaks, scampi, etc., at bar. Thirty cheeses available. *Special drinks* Draught Guinness. *Route* Off A4. *Nearest station* Langley. *Telephone* Colnbrook 2628.

Colnbrook is an old village, by-passed by both time and the Bath Road, which curves away north of it. It is by no means a forgotten village, how-ever, and the travellers that have passed through it, or put up in one of the many inns, read like a pageant of English history.

It lies on the extreme edge of Buckinghamshire, and indeed the old bridge over the Colne bears the county boundary-stone and the date 1777. For a great many years it was the only passable road between London and Windsor and as a result had more royal travellers through it than any village in England.

It was therefore natural that it should have more inns than most, and the five that still exist represent only a small fraction of the number origin-ally standing. The oldest of these (and the fourth oldest in England) is still there. This is The Ostrich, a fine half-timbered building on three sides of a square, with a history going back to 1106. King John is said to have stayed here before signing the Magna Carta at near-by Runnymede, though not in this building, which dates from about 1400. But this is old enough to have seen a good deal of history, and The Ostrich was already old when Queen Elizabeth stayed at Colnbrook for the night in 1558. This, however, was not one of her famous and splendid 'progresses'. On this occasion she was a prisoner on her way from Woodstock to captivity in Hampton Court.

Foreign ambassadors and notabilities, proceeding to Windsor for a royal audience, used The Ostrich as a robing-room before embarking on the last stage of the journey, whilst Colnbrook was a convenient night-stop for merchants and travellers of every kind along the Bath road. It is small wonder, therefore, that vagabonds and highwaymen gave Colnbrook a good deal of attention. The pickings were fat, and the stretch of road between Colnbrook and Longford became almost as notorious as Hounslow Heath.

Inevitably there were occasions when unscrupulous landlords co-operated with robbers and highwaymen, and for many years the landlord of The Ostrich went one step further and organised things for his own benefit before the customer had left the inn. A bed in one of the rooms, reserved for the more wealthy merchant, was ingeniously placed on top of a trap-door. Late at night, when the occupant would be sleeping-off the effect of several quarts of beer and an enormous supper, a lever was pulled and the trap-door would swivel over, pitching the unfortunate sleeper into a cauldron of boiling water placed strategically in the kitchen below.

It is not known how many murders were committed in this way, the figure varies from thirteen to sixty, but the landlord and his wife were eventually caught and both were hanged. For the benefit of any present-day visitors who may be thinking of opening a guest-house, a working model of this interesting contrivance is displayed in the bar.

With this history of murder and violence, The Ostrich can be expected to have its fair share of ghost stories. But the only thing that seems to have affected its popularity was a rumour, about 1800, that a curse had been put on the beer by a gipsy who had been refused a drink, and that anybody sampling the brew would soon die! This is certainly not the situation today. It is a very busy inn, and many have said that after an evening there they have never felt better in their lives!

CRYER'S HILL

The White Lion

Brewer Courage. *Food* Snacks. *Route* A4128. *Nearest station* High Wycombe. *Telephone* Holmer Green 2303.

The road from High Wycombe to Great Missenden (A4128) is a good cross-section of Buckinghamshire history and Buckinghamshire scenery.

It leaves High Wycombe by way of the busy Frogmoor junction with the A40, and is very soon threading the beautiful Hughenden Valley. After two miles or so, past Hughenden Park and Manor, the road turns right up Cryer's Hill and enters country which is different but no less attractive than the valley below.

At the top of Cryer's Hill is The White Lion. Externally, perhaps, it is no very imposing. Inside, however, the atmosphere is one of cosiness and comfort. It is a surprise to find how old The White Lion really is. The beams are low, but there is plenty of space to move around. Both saloon and public-bars are of reasonable size, and the counter itself is long enough to accommodate a respectable number of drinkers. The beer is Courage's.

Outside, there is a good car-park, and a garden behind. There is also a superb view across the Hughenden Valley to the wooded hills beyond Hughenden Manor, once the home of Benjamin Disraeli and his 'perfect wife' can just be seen, and on certain evenings one can hear the bells of the little church just by the house, where the great statesman and his wife sleep in peace.

There are several pubs on the High Wycombe–Great Missenden Road all of them pleasant. It is not only the view that gives The White Lion the edge on the others.

DATCHET

The Royal Stag

Brewer Friary Meux. *Food* Snacks. *Route* A331. *Nearest station* Datchet *Telephone* Datchet 618.

Datchet is just about as far south as you can get in Buckinghamshire. The county boundary follows the winding course of the Thames from Medmenham in the west to Datchet and Wraysbury in the east, and here the river takes a turn south as it leaves Buckinghamshire and flows on to London and the sea.

The Royal Stag is a handsome Georgian building near the church in the centre of this pleasant riverside village. The brewers are Friary Meux, a company whose pubs are not met very often in Buckinghamshire. The Royal Stag is a snug sort of place, obviously popular with local residents but also attracting the passer-by from its position facing the village green.

It is usual to find beams and solid timber in old pubs. It is less usual to find the walls entirely covered with the sides and lids of old wine chests, as here It is a pleasant method of decoration, interesting yet not obtrusive, though a little overpowering until you get used to it.

Boating and fishing are the chief attractions of Datchet. With Eton College close at hand it is not surprising that Izaak Walton fished here often, in company with his good friend Sir Henry Wootton, Provost of Eton. Royal anglers, too, have fished at Datchet, notably Charles II. Pope, concise and to the point as usual, wrote about this:

> Methinks I see our mighty monarch stand
> The pliant rod now trembling in his hand;
> And see he now doth up from Datchet come,
> Laden, with spoils of slaughter'd gudgeons, home.

DENHAM

The Dog & Duck

Brewer Wethered. *Food* Snacks. *Route* A4020. *Nearest station* Uxbridge. *Telephone* Uxbridge 37241.

The old road from London to Oxford crosses the boundary between Middlesex and Buckinghamshire just west of Uxbridge. The boundary is the River Colne, and almost the first pub in Buckinghamshire is The Dog & Duck.

It is a seventeenth-century inn and marks the site of the old turnpike on that busy road. The small saloon and larger public have been renovated, but some beams of the original structure can still be seen.

This is not an 'Olde-worlde' pub, although some character is kept through the wonderful collection of genuine and rare horse-brasses collected by the licensee. At the same time it is not aggressively modern, the improvements having been carried out mainly to ease the work behind the bar rather than to benefit the customers.

The house belongs to Wethered of Marlow, and is notable for the fact that unlike most wayside inns it has no swinging sign. Instead it has a plaster relief, on the front wall, showing a dog chasing a duck.

This part of Denham is called New Denham, and The Dog & Duck serves the large housing estate off the main road as well as the casual passer-by. But it is very much a 'local', and like most 'locals' is a friendly place for the stranger to visit.

The turnpike near it was called the 'half-penny gate' as this was the amount of the toll. Though the days of the turnpikes are gone, more money changes hands on the spot these days than ever did before. It takes a good many half-pennies to buy a pint today, but they are handed over very much more willingly.

DENHAM VILLAGE

The Falcon

Brewer Wethered. *Bedrooms* 6. *Food* Snacks at the bar. *Nearest station* Denham. *Telephone* Denham 2125.

In the angle formed by the roaring A40 road to Oxford and the fast road to Rickmansworth, Denham village lies untouched and unspoilt in the middle of the suburban development around. The old houses and inns, the little village green and the old parish church form a little jewel in this flat and uninspiring section of Buckinghamshire, and Pinewood Studios, not far away, frequently takes advantage of its beauty when seeking an 'old-English' atmosphere.

The Falcon catches the eye at once, in the middle of many eye-catching buildings. What might otherwise be a rather severe front is relieved by a double flight of stone steps with iron railings leading to the quaint public-bar. The many window-boxes are ablaze with colour in summer, and even in such a picturesque setting The Falcon stands out as a building of character.

The name perpetuates the ancient sport of falconry, and puts the date of this inn in the early sixteen-hundreds. The little River Misbourne, after its journey past Amersham and the Chalfonts, runs through Denham before joining the Colne below Denham Court.

It is a peaceful place most of the time, and always picturesque. Less than half an hour from London it is a favourite with the motorist, and parking can become a problem late in the evening. So go early, whilst the ramblers and the wistaria on the mellow brick buildings can still be seen, and before The Falcon gets so busy that you have to drink your beer on the stone steps outside.

DROPMORE

The Jolly Woodman

Brewer Wethered. *Food* Snacks. *Telephone* Farnham Common 350.

A mile south of Beaconsfield, on the B473, a right-hand fork leads to Burnham. This road, twisting and turning, up-hill and down, takes one into a remote area of woodland, of sudden views between high hedges, and progressively away from what is called civilisation. Hardly a house is passed for two miles, until suddenly, in a clearing, we see The Jolly Woodman on the left lying a little back from the road.

And indeed, this is a jolly pub and lives up to its name. It is, of course, extremely ancient, but like all ancient pubs takes it for granted and is quite unselfconscious about it. The two little bars are cosy, and the counter in between, serving both of them, seems to co-ordinate the company into one cheerful whole. It is impossible to be neglected or to feel 'out-of-it' in The Jolly Woodman. For many years it was a stop for the coach journeying between Burnham and Beaconsfield, and advertised 'Provender for man and beast'. It still provides the 'provender' though there are few 'beasts' these days.

In one curious respect, however, The Jolly Woodman still gives priority to the 'man' rather than to his companion, whether a beast or a member of what is laughingly termed 'the weaker sex'. It is one of the few pubs where the 'Ladies' is outside and the 'Gents' inside. There is a moral here somewhere, if one has that sort of mind!

However, The Jolly Woodman makes both sexes more than welcome within, and dispenses Wethered's beer with efficiency and gusto. A popular spot, particularly at week-ends, it is just as well it is alone in a forest glade. The laughter ringing out into the night might not be appreciated in a built-up area, and more than one bird, asleep in its nest, has been known to transfer to another branch next day.

DUNSMORE

The Fox

Brewer Aylesbury Brewery Co. *Food* Snacks at bar. *Special drinks* Ind Coope's Bitter and Mild, Draught Guinness, Watney's Red Barrel. *Route* Off A413. *Nearest station* Wendover. *Telephone* Wendover 3186.

Once off the main road in the Chilterns and it is surprisingly easy to get lost. The twisting lanes and narrow 'bottoms' of the area round Frieth and Hambleden are notoriously confusing, and the countryside immediately south of Wendover, in which Dunsmore lies, is little better. A finger-post on the A413, a mile-and-a-half west of Wendover points the way to Dunsmore. The lane runs due west, over the railway, then climbs, twisting and turning and becoming even narrower as it nears the village. It is only a mile from the main road—but it can seem a very long mile.

Although Dunsmore is a tiny place, hidden in the wooded slopes of the Chilterns, The Fox has almost succeeded in hiding itself from the village. A right turn at the narrow cross-roads leads you finally to the car-park—an indication that you are not by any means the first white man to have penetrated thus far. On the contrary, The Fox is an extremely popular old pub. All the usual characteristics are present—the old beams, the big fireplace, the cosy bars—but there are in addition some less usual features. An impressive collection of Kennel Club certificates adorns the walls, and enquiries reveal that miniature dachsunds are grown on the premises.

There is a pleasant garden, complete with a miniature golf-course, and most surprising of all, a donkey called Lucifer who is partial to gin and well on the way to being a founder-member of Equine Alcoholics.

All in all The Fox has a great deal to commend it. It is an Aylesbury Brewery Company pub, and it is worth remembering that it sells pipe tobacco. Despite his name the talented Lucifer does not smoke as well as drink gin, but no doubt he will get round to this in time.

EAST BURNHAM

The Stag

Brewer Wethered. *Bedrooms* 5. *Food* Large snack-bar serving grills. *Nearest station* Burnham. *Telephone* Farnham Common 26.

One of the chief glories of Buckinghamshire lies in its beech-woods, which at one time covered the whole of the county. Few large areas of woodland remain, but one of the most impressive is Burnham Beeches. The three hundred acres of these lovely woods were saved for posterity by the Corporation of the City of London who, in 1878, bought the area for preservation as a public open space.

East Burnham Common, which adjoins the Beeches, lies a mile or so west of the Slough–Beaconsfield road (B473), and on the edge of the common we find The Stag. It is a large, Victorian-looking building, standing its own, with little danger of so-called 'development' affecting it.

Internally it has an enormous bar, with a snack-bar adjoining, and an entertaining collection of motoring bric-à-brac adds to the colour. For The Stag is a mecca for the car-rally types and vintage-car enthusiasts. Old horns, lamps, number-plates and photographs of cars abound, and the clientèle tends to be the younger enthusiast rather than the oldest inhabitant.

It is a Wethered house, and tactfully does bed-and-breakfast for the benefit of any addict whose vintage model has less enthusiasm than its owner. This seems an unlikely eventuality, as most spares required appear to be adorning the walls. The Stag is certainly a pub with a difference. But if, after a visit, you return to your car and find the steering-wheel missing, don't be alarmed. You will probably find it hanging up in the bar, being gloated over by enthusiasts!

FORD

The Dinton Hermit

Brewer Aylesbury Brewery Co. *Food* Restaurant. *Special drinks* Ind Coope's Bitter and Mild, Draught Guinness, Watney's Red Barrel. *Nearest station* Aylesbury. *Telephone* Stone 379.

Half-way between Aylesbury and Thame the tiny village of Ford lies jus
south of the old main road which runs between the two towns in an almos
straight line.

It is a secluded spot set in the Vale of Aylesbury, with the chalk edge o
the Chilterns looking like a line of cliffs to the south.

The Dinton Hermit is a fifteenth-century stone building, good lookin
and solid and quite content to be away from the main road and the roar o
traffic. It belongs to the Aylesbury Brewery Company and despite it
seclusion (or, more likely, because of it) it is a popular pub with Aylesbur
people. There is a good garden, and in addition to the Watney's and In
Coope's beer, grills are provided, with a surprisingly good selection o
wines.

The hermit who gave the pub its name was one John Bigg, born in 159
at Dinton two miles away. He became clerk to Simon Mayne of Dinton
friend of Cromwell and one of the judges who passed sentence on Charles I
Tradition says that John Bigg was actually the King's executioner, bu
this has never been established. He was a good scholar and a man o
some wealth, but the events leading to the Restoration and the imprison
ment of his employer in 1660 affected his brain, and he became a recluse
retiring to a cave and living on charity. His faculties were not too impaired
however, for him to neglect the more important things of life, and we ar
told that he always carried three bottles on his girdle, one for strong bee
one for small beer and one for milk.

The inn-sign is a painting of this disillusioned man, looking surpris
ingly fit despite his tribulations. Which seems to prove that thoug
kings and governments may fall, life is still bearable if you can get you
beer.

FORTY GREEN, near Beaconsfield

The Royal Standard of England

Free House. Food Snacks at bar (cheese and chutney). *Special drinks* 'Ow
Roger' Beer, Worthington E, Flowers'. *Nearest station* Beaconsfield
Telephone Beaconsfield 2756.

orty Green is not an easy place to find, tucked away in the fold of the hills ·oss-country between Beaconsfield and Penn. And even when you have egotiated the twisting and narrow lanes that eventually reach this little amlet, The Royal Standard of England may still elude you. But not for •ng. It is a pub that is known the world over, and is unique in more than ne respect. Externally it has the appearance of a fifteenth-century timbered ouse and looks quite unlike a normal village inn. Internally it is even more nusual, with its curved and bulging wooden walls more like a ship than a ub, massive oak beams and uneven floor. Antiques and curios abound, and if this were not enough the main rooms are lit only by candle and oil- mp.

It has been a pub a long time, and three hundred years ago was called `he Ship'. Its present name is claimed to be unique in the country and, true 1ough, it does possess a Royal Standard, that of Edward VII.

This is a free house, selling various draught and bottled beers, and also s own black and potent Burton brew known as 'Owd Roger'. This is ightening stuff, and should be treated with the utmost respect, bearing in ind the tortuous journey back before you regain the main road, and the ventieth century.

ULMER

he Black Horse

rewer Courage. *Food* Snacks at bar. *Nearest station* Gerrards Cross. *Telephone* ulmer 83.

ulmer is one of those little villages just south of the A40 which seems ntouched by time, and half asleep with its memories. It is on the Gerrards ross to Wexham road, nestling at the bottom of a valley, with a steep pproach either side. Fulmer is tiny—some fine Georgian properties, the 1urch, a shop, the village post-office and The Black Horse make up its uildings—but it is peaceful. The Black Horse is next door to the church, 1d is a low, half-timbered building set back from the road. The church is rly seventeenth century, and The Black Horse was already there when it vas built, as the inn was used as a hostel by the masons.

Today it is one of the many picturesque old inns with which this part of Buckinghamshire is so well blessed, each having its own individual character. It is a Courage house, and all the beer is from the wood, a characteristic which is becoming less and less common.

The landlord has accumulated a vast collection of matchbox tops (some 6000 or so) and has in addition a very fine set of tankards adorning the wall. As a change from the familiar 'ship-in-bottle' found in seaside pubs, The Black Horse has, appropriately, a black horse in a bottle! It is not all that far from Pinewood Studios, and is a favourite with more than one famous actor when filming there. But even if the company is not star studded, the three bars are comfortable and the conversation entertaining. If, by any chance, you also happen to produce a matchbox not already in the collection you will receive treatment which would make any star's publicity agent green with envy.

GEORGE GREEN

The Double Century

Brewer Harman. *Food* Grills and snacks. *Special drinks* Draught Guinness, Tavern Keg. *Route* A412. *Nearest station* Slough. *Telephone* Slough 28759.

This is an attractive and modern pub, two miles out of Slough on the Uxbridge road (A412). It was built in 1963 and derives its name from being the two hundredth pub opened by Messrs. Harman, the Uxbridge brewers. It is now part of the great Courage empire, and an extremely good example of modern pub architecture and design. There is a good car park, both front and rear, and a pleasant garden at the side. The two large bars are most attractively decorated, well lit, and comfortably furnished. As well as Tavern Keg, I.P.A. Bitter and Mild, there is also Draught Guinness to be had, together with an astonishing array of grills and snacks.

One cannot help feeling that brewers' architects are often on happier ground when designing a new pub, than when restoring an old one. Here, at any rate, they have succeeded in providing both atmosphere and comfort haracteristics which, unfortunately, are not always found together in nodern pubs today.

GERRARDS CROSS

The Bull

ree House. Bedrooms 33. *Food* Restaurant and grill-room. *Special drinks*)raught Bass, Draught Tolley, Draught Flowers'. *Nearest station* Beacons-ield. *Telephone* Gerrards Cross 2005.

3etween Tatling End and Beaconsfield the A40 trunk road to Wales runs hrough an area of common land and pines. This is the southern tip of 3errards Cross, and it needs little imagination to picture this stretch of road wo hundred years ago as a very suitable venue for highwaymen.

The Bull was there then as a coaching-inn, and was built in 1688. A amous highwayman of the time was Jack Shrimpton, a name still found n the district, and when the pace became a little too hot the landlord of The 3ull frequently 'obliged' by providing shelter and refuge in the rambling orridors and many rooms of the inn.

The Bull

Today The Bull still caters for the passing traveller, and does it with great efficiency. The main bar is an attractive mixture of beams, oak posts and pleasant furnishings, and contains an interesting collection of 'Spy' cartoons of eminent or notorious Victorian worthies. Shrimpton was hanged at Tyburn in 1713 despite the landlord of The Bull, and perhaps it is to make belated amends that the bar is called The Shrimpton Room.

In addition there is a graceful cocktail-bar, and a magnificent dining-room.

The Bull is a free house, and dispenses Bass, Tolley and Flowers' draught beers. The beer-pumps themselves are curious, being worked by foot and not by hand.

It is, of course, an hotel, and a very popular one. Highwaymen are rarely seen in The Bull these days. One is more likely to gaze in awed admiration at a film star with friend, as Pinewood Studios are little more than a reel's length away.

GIBRALTAR

The Bottle & Glass

Brewer Aylesbury Brewery Co. *Food* Snacks at the bar. *Special drinks* Ind Coope's Bitter and Mild, Draught Guinness, Watney's Red Barrel. *Nearest station* Aylesbury. *Telephone* Stone 488.

A mile or so past Dinton, on the Aylesbury–Thame road, The Bottle & Glass sits by the roadside. It looks inviting, with its dormer windows peeping out from under the thatch and the two long benches on each side of the door.

Since 1420 the building has been there. Like so many other wayside inns it was originally cottages, but has held a licence for at least three hundred years.

The great old oven of one of the cottages can be seen in the bar, and the long shovel used for getting out the bread.

Gibraltar is one of the many odd place-names found in the county. It is part of Dinton parish, and just north of this village is the extraordinary mock castle built in 1769 by Sir John Vanhattan to show off his collection of fossils. This is a good place to have a picnic and to wander around among the firs. It passes the afternoon until The Bottle & Glass opens.

GREAT MISSENDEN

The George

Brewer Aylesbury Brewery Co. *Food* Snacks—soup at lunch-time. *Special drinks* Ind Coope's Bitter and Mild, Draught Guinness, Watney's Red Barrel. *Route* A413. *Nearest station* Great Missenden. *Telephone* Great Missenden 2084.

Not many pubs are of as genuine an antiquity as The George. It stands in the narrowest part of the High Street, facing Church Street, and has been standing there since 1480.

The old coach arch at the side of the house leads into a courtyard, now the car-park, the south side of which is bounded by a most attractive sixteenth-century building. This is a two-storeyed and half-timbered construction, with the characteristic projecting upper storey and protruding beams of its time, and was formerly the Missenden court-house.

The George has only one bar—but what a lot there is in it! The structure of this ancient building can well be seen in the woodwork. The ancient beams are intricately carved, sections of seventeenth-century Bible boxes are on view, together with such comparatively modern items as rush-light holders and straw splitters.

At the side of the bar is the lounge, equally old, and containing a selection of good Victoriana. No china dogs here, but figures of Queen Victoria and Prince Albert at the time of their wedding, sharing the mantelpiece with, of all people, Moody and Sankey!

The drink available is not only 'water bright from the crystal spring'. The George belongs to the Aylesbury Brewery Company, who are connected with Ind Coope. Good draught bitter and cider from the wood are supplied. Snacks at any time, together with soup at midday cheer the traveller on his way. I am sure Moody and Sankey would have approved!

GREAT MISSENDEN

The Nag's Head

Brewer Aylesbury Brewery Co. *Food* Restaurant—grills, scampi, whitebait
Special drinks Ind Coope's Bitter and Mild, Draught Guinness, Watney'
Red Barrel. *Route* A413. *Nearest station* Great Missenden. *Telephone* Grea
Missenden 2945.

The Great Missenden By-pass cuts out (as it is intended to do) a pleasan
Buckinghamshire village and half a dozen or so pubs.

From the direction of Amersham the old road comes off the by-pass to th
left soon after the railway-bridge. Half a mile or less brings us to The Nag'
Head, on the corner of Nag's Head Lane.

It is an old pub, renovated rather than modernised, in a way which
retains the charm of the original building but adds to the comfort. Th
saloon-bar, on the left, is a split-level affair, the higher plane being use
mainly for those who wish to eat. Down three steps and you are in the les
rarefied atmosphere of the bar proper, gazing into the eyes of one of th
many attractive young ladies who take turns in dishing out the booze.

It is difficult to know whether this old pub attracts the younger elemen
because of the staff, or whether the girls like working there because of th
young men. The fact remains that a high proportion of the clientèle consist
of keen young executives rapidly learning how to become tired business
men. It may, of course, be because of the food, which is good and imagina
tive (Dorset Knobs and whitebait among other things), or because of th
beer, which is Benskin's and Watney's.

The public-bar is split-level in a different sort of way, having a run-up
to the dart-board and a floor which ensures your hitting your head on
beam as you move towards your drink. For some odd reason it is assume
that safety-matches have not yet been invented, and ignition is provided b
a pile of Swan Vestas and a rough brick!

There is a good car-park at the rear, sometimes filled to capacity with
vintage-cars plus enthusiasts, who meet regularly here.

Though perhaps not the ideal place for an intimate chat with the girl
friend, The Nag's Head is an entertaining place. It has character, like mos

old pubs, and is none the worse for having extra character and entertainment provided by its customers.

HARTWELL, near Aylesbury

The Bugle Horn

Brewer Ind Coope. *Food* Restaurant (large) lunches and dinners. *Special drinks* Draught Double Diamond. *Route* A418. *Nearest station* Aylesbury. *Telephone* Stone 407.

The great wall of Hartwell Park runs for over a mile by the side of the Aylesbury to Thame road (A418). Hartwell House, within the Park, is remembered mainly for its years of fame between 1809 and 1814, when it housed the unlucky Louis XVIII of France and his family. The wall turns sharply some two miles from Aylesbury, following the road as it enters the little village. At this bend, standing foursquare and solid, The Bugle Horn looks down the road to Aylesbury, as if to make sure that it is not going to be missed.

This is a spacious old house, well restored and attractive inside and out. The modernisation has been carried out with taste, both in the elegant saloon-bar and in the sherry-bar. Polished wood, wrought-iron, good carpeting

The Bugle Horn

and sense of space are the main impressions in The Bugle Horn. The occasional appearance of girls in red hunting-jackets takes a bit of getting used to. These are waitresses from the restaurant, dressed in keeping with the hunting tradition of this old inn.

The gardens are immense and very much bigger than the car-park, itself not small.

King Louis, if he ever took a walk outside the grounds of Hartwell House, would no doubt have appreciated the company at The Bugle Horn. It is unfortunate that his timing was slightly out and he returned to France a few days after the news of Napoleon's escape from Elba! He would have been far better off at Hartwell, and far more comfortable in The Bugle Horn.

HAWRIDGE COMMON

The Full Moon

Brewer Wethered. *Food* Snacks at bar. *Nearest station* Chesham. *Telephone* Cholesbury 262.

South Buckinghamshire is not noted for its extensive views or wide horizons. Except where the Chiltern Hills drop suddenly to the Vale of Aylesbury the little lanes keep to the valleys, and only the occasional gaps between the high hedges give sudden and fleeting glimpses of the country around.

Hawridge Common, some three miles due north of Chesham, is a pleasant exception to this. It is on a ridge, 600 feet up, with cottages lining the road one side and fields falling away to the Hertfordshire border on the other. In the middle of the cottages is The Full Moon, a pub since 1760 and originally five cottages built a century before. For nearly a hundred years it was known as The Half Moon, and though the reason for the change is unknown the present name is one that is very rarely met.

It is a low, rambling pub, the main bar supplying the needs of the local trade whilst visitors tend to favour the odd little room adjoining which consists almost entirely of an enormous ingle-nook.

The Common is a perfect playground for children and The Full Moon, bearing this in mind, has provided a special annexe for them alongside the

118

The Full Moon

building named, rather archly, Kids Korner. In addition there is a delightful garden, with the added attraction of a bowling-green for the energetic.

The outside wall of The Full Moon bears an interesting firemark of 1765, a relic of the days when fire-brigades contracted to put out only the fires of their own subscribers, leaving the others to burn.

These days the licensee suffers a hazard against which there is no insurance. Car-rally organisers hear of the pub with glee, wetting their pencils as they realise the possibilities of the name. It is a pity that Sunday afternoons is the favourite time for these capers. The remarks of the landlord on being wakened for the twentieth time and asked if he is the 'Man in the Moon' are no part of this book.

HEDGERLEY

The One Pin

Brewer Courage. *Food* Snacks (very large sandwiches) at **bar.** *Special drinks* Tavern Keg. *Nearest station* Gerrards Cross. *Telephone* Farnham Common 135.

A mile south of Hedgerley a winding lane runs across country, from the Slough–Gerrards Cross road (A332) to the Slough–Beaconsfield road (B473). At the cross-roads stands The One Pin, solid and important looking, making very sure that it is noticed. Many village inns in this rural part of Buckinghamshire have suffered the doubtful advantages of 'restoration'. The One Pin has survived any effort to superimpose additional 'character' on its pleasant exterior, and inside the feeling of being in a truly ancient hostelry is very apparent.

Although comparatively remote, this pub always seems to be busy. No doubt its good position accounts for this to a certain extent, but in addition it is a friendly place which, having once been found, is easy to find again.

The two bars are large and comfortable, with low ceilings criss-crossed by old rafters. Outside there is plenty of room to park, and, as seems inevitable in this area, the talk is largely of cars.

Hedgerley village, just up the road, remains remote despite a large housing estate near by. According to Alison Uttley a spot near here is called 'Wapses', spelt Wapseys on the Ordnance Survey map, which also shows a district known as Egypt. With names like these the traveller may well be confused, and perhaps it is just as well that The One Pin, with its Courage sign and 'pin' barrel hanging outside, is in such a strategic and easily remembered position.

HIGH WYCOMBE

The Falcon

Free House. Bedrooms 11. *Food* Restaurant and snacks at bar. *Special drinks* Mann's I.P.A. and Mild, Watney's Red Barrel. Port and sherry from the cask. *Route* A40. *Nearest station* High Wycombe. *Telephone* High Wycombe 126.

Despite its name, High Wycombe (as William Cobbett pointed out) runs for about three miles along the bottom of a deep valley. The traveller along the London–Oxford road (A40) has plenty of time to ponder on this phenomenon, and to look around him, as he slowly progresses westwards. The wide and attractive High Street, always busy with shoppers and traffic, terminates in a cluster of old buildings, reducing the street to a narrow gap.

The eighteenth-century Guildhall faces the crawling traffic one side of the road, the charming octagonal market hall stands back on the right. Tucked in to the left of the Guildhall is The Falcon. The angle between the two buildings consists of a tiny car-park.

It is said that part of the cellars of The Falcon date back to 1384. The Dickensian atmosphere of this inn is due to a discovery made in these cellars in 1950. This consisted of a series of wood carvings of Dickens characters made at the end of last century by a local craftsman who, it seems, was unable to settle his bill! Although the carvings are no longer there, their discovery is perpetuated in the snug 'Pickwick' bar, with its sketches of Bumble, the Fat Boy, Oliver Twist, and others. The long and pleasant saloon-bar is not so Dickensian. However, it makes up for this with pleasant wood panelling, sporting prints and views of Wycombe in the eighteenth century. Tucked in a corner to the left of the bar is an odd set of etchings to find in a pub. They are the Hogarth 'Four Stages of Cruelty', and the squeamish are advised not to examine them too closely before eating! You can, however, fortify yourself suitably beforehand with Mann's I.P.A. or Mild draught beers, or Red Barrel. Port and sherry are supplied direct from the cask. There is therefore really no excuse for not looking at the 'Four Stages' and sampling at least one of the fifty-six varieties of sandwiches which are available.

HIGH WYCOMBE

The White Lion

Brewer Aylesbury Brewery Co. *Food* Snacks. *Special drinks* Ind Coope's Bitter and Mild, Draught Guinness, Watney's Red Barrel. *Route* A404. *Nearest station* High Wycombe. *Telephone* High Wycombe 910.

Despite various recessions in the furniture trade High Wycombe remains a thriving and prosperous town. As a result shop-sites are at a premium and frontage on a busy road is a valuable asset.

The White Lion, in Crendon Street, is almost next to the station in one of the busiest parts of the town. No doubt it is for this reason that the owners, the Aylesbury Brewery Company, have rebuilt the pub and used

most of the valuable frontage as a window for the off-sales department. No
doubt this is good business, but there must be many who hurry by not
realising that the door at the side of the shop leads into a very pleasant
modern pub.

It is not a big place. The saloon-bar at the front is adequate, and the small
curved counter ensures that the barman can serve practically everybody
without moving from the one spot. This also ensures a rapid continuation of
supplies for the customer, a satisfactory arrangement all round.

Good carpets, and furniture made by a famous local firm provide a
mellow atmosphere despite the newness. Nothing is brash in this place
although it is one of the most modern pubs in Wycombe.

In the same way the public-bar is worlds away from what we are accustomed to in town pubs. It is bright and light, and the bar seems more suitable
for the dispensing of cocktails rather than pints of mild-and-bitter. Still, this
is a good thing. The tendency in latter years for brewers to do away with
public-bars and enlarge the saloon is an idea that can have unfortunate
repercussions. Often not only do the public-bar customers vanish, but the
'improvements' to the saloon result in a vast room of negative character
doing nothing to please the regular customers or to attract new ones.

HIGH WYCOMBE

Ye Exchange

Brewer Aylesbury Brewery Co. *Food* Salami and other sandwiches at bar.
Special drinks Ind Coope's Bitter and Mild, Draught Guinness, Watney's
Red Barrel. *Route* A40. *Nearest station* High Wycombe. *Telephone* High
Wycombe 446.

If you like draught cider you will like Ye Exchange. And if you are partial
to American servicemen then this definitely is the place for you.

There are at least four types of cider and an even greater variety of
Americans, who come from the U.S. base up Marlow Hill. The trans-
atlantic influence probably accounts for the fact that this is one pub at least
where there is no shortage of ice.

It is one of the two Aylesbury Brewery Company pubs in the town, and stands on the main A40 road just west of the turning to Hughenden. Its flat and not very inspiring front lies several feet back from the pavement, presumably on what will be the new building line in centuries to come.

It replaces an older pub on the site, and inside the architects have used a clever combination of wood and glass. The long, straight counter stretches the full width of the bar, and the subdued lighting and good modern furniture give character to what might otherwise be just a rectangular room. Additional character is provided by the two licensees, bearing the unlikely name of Plato and known far and wide as The Battling Brothers. The technique with which they supply the wants of their customers is highly individual and if, around the streets of Wycombe, you meet an American with permanently raised eyebrows and a dazed look the chances are he will have just come from Ye Exchange.

The secret is never to take anything seriously in this place—except, of course, your change. And beware of the cider. After a few glasses of this you may well find that you have put down a deposit on a couple of eight-day clocks or a fur coat. The following morning you will wish most fervently for some of that ice you left behind.

HOLTSPUR, near Beaconsfield

The King's Head

Brewer Courage. *Food* Restaurant. *Route* A40. *Nearest station* Beaconsfield. *Telephone* Beaconsfield 337.

This old inn is difficult to miss, standing as it does right by the side of the A40 between Beaconsfield and High Wycombe. It is at the top of the long hill running down into the approaches of Wycombe, and opposite the branch road to Wooburn and Bourne End (B4440).

It is a four-square sort of place, with an easy car-park one side and a delightful rose garden on the other. It is of seventeenth-century construction and the public-bar, with its enormous fireplace, was originally two cottages adjoining the pub. The saloon-lounge is most attractive, the accent being predominantly wood panelling, with a long and low window-seat from which one may gaze pityingly at the scurrying A40 traffic.

A carved wooden arch leads into the comfortable dining-room, and the whole atmosphere is one of solidity and well-being.

This is a Courage house selling, amongst other beers, their well-known Directors' Bitter. The dining-room also manages to incorporate quite a lot of alcohol into the fare, and offers such unusual delicacies as Gaelic coffee and Royal coffee. In a more solid form scampi with brandy and cream will ensure your quota, even if you don't get to the bar. But you will!

IBSTONE

The Fox

Brewer Wethered. *Food* Snacks at bar. Coffee always available. *Telephone* Turville Heath 389.

Half a mile from Stokenchurch on the Oxford side a lane branches off the A40 and disappears into the beechwoods. It is an unassuming lane, high on the edge of the Chilterns, to start with, then dropping gradually until it meets its sisters from Turville and Fingest four or five miles on.

There is little to disturb the peace of this lane. Houses are few, and Ibstone and The Fox form the only break in this rural and leafy way.

Even The Fox stands a little back, as if to avoid any suggestion of commercial intrusion.

It is an old country pub, picturesque and inviting, quiet during the winter months but in the summer an oasis for cricketers on Ibstone Common. The interior woodwork is new, and very well done, and the long, low seats round the walls encourage conversation and induce a feeling of relaxation. The large and modern stone fireplace is, perhaps, not quite such a happy idea in this setting, though it gives a focal point to the room.

Wethered are the brewers here, and obviously their architects have given a great deal of thought to the redesigning of this old pub. The public-bar contains two enormous old wood settles, and in this room the original structure of the building can still be seen. Most customers at The Fox have come from a distance, and it is therefore natural that a good variety of snacks is available. Even coffee is provided without a murmur, served at the handsome, wood-panelled counter, where the landlord listens to the inquest on the match—and tactfully refrains from umpiring.

LANE END

The Clayton Arms

Brewer Watney. *Food* Snacks. *Special drinks* Mann's Draught Bitter. *Route* B482. *Nearest station* High Wycombe. *Telephone* Lane End 269.

The Fire of London in 1666, as the Plague before it, altered the pattern of life in the metropolis. Many people moved out of the City of London into the countryside around, meaning to return when things were back to normal. But things never did get back to normal—and many never came to live in London again.

Such a one was Sir Robert Clayton, an influential City merchant, who at the time of the Fire decided that the clean air of Buckinghamshire was more to his taste. He chose the hamlet of Lane End, and there built a manor-house on ground that he bought.

That manor-house is today The Clayton Arms, a brick building at the Marlow end of the village. It looks more like a domestic building than an inn, though internally it has been adapted for the more serious pastime of drinking. Even so one still has rather the feeling of drinking in a private house, but this in no way detracts from its charm and character.

It is a Watney house, with Mann's bitter on draught and the ubiquitous Red Barrel from the keg.

Sir Robert, himself no mean drinker, would have been glad to know his name lives on in Lane End in this way.

LANGLEY

The Merrymakers MEADOW ROAD

Brewer Wethered. *Food* Snacks. *Route* Off A4. *Nearest station* Langley. *Telephone* Slough 41266.

Though Wethered's have been brewing beer in Marlow for over two hundred years nobody could accuse them of not moving with the times. The Merrymakers was built in 1964 and has the sort of modernity which never jars and, one feels, will never date.

It is situated on a vast estate at Langley, and though only a short distance from the Bath road (A4) is not all that easily accessible. Roads on council estates are notorious for looking alike, and though The Merrymakers is a most striking-looking building it can also prove to be very elusive. This being so it is not surprising that it has little passing trade and draws its customers from the hundreds of houses and flats all round it.

There are two very large bars in this very large pub, both most attractively decorated. The old-time music-hall provides the motif in the public-bar, with an enormous 'blow-up' of the inside of one of these establishments taking up most of one wall. An attractive touch is the decoration of the beer-pump handles, each carrying a charming coloured illustration of a well-known pantomime character.

The lounge is not quite as large as the public-bar, but again the decorations are original. The lighting is more restrained and the motif here is the word 'Merrymakers'. This has been neatly developed by the use of reproductions of the famous series of paintings by Breughel, and in fact the sign outside the pub is from the same source. The architects have used some pleasant

126

deas in seating. Normally one finds a combination of bench seats round the walls, with scattered tables and chairs in the middle of the room. Here the benches have been extended, back-to-back, right into the room thus giving maximum seating accommodation without taking up too much floor space. It has also been assumed that many customers will want to lean against the bar, and a broad foot-rail has therefore been provided. Though this may seem a small point, the absence of a foot-rail is an unfortunate feature of many modern pubs.

The music-hall atmosphere of the public-bar is no accident, for this pub is unusual in having a large theatre on the premises. The reason for this is that the building was designed in conjunction with the wishes of the Langley Community Association. Next to the lounge a door leads to another bar and to the theatre, where dances, bingo sessions and the like go on at week-ends.

Without doubt The Merrymakers is a most interesting building, and very well-designed. Except for one thing. It is all very well providing two bars each big enough to hold three hundred people—but why make the conveniences so small that only three people can use them at a time? You can't interfere with Nature!

LINSLADE

The Globe Inn

Free House. Food Snacks. *Special drinks* Worthington E, Flowers' Keg, Draught Guinness, Watney's Red Barrel, Draught Tolley, Watney's Bitter, Flowers' Bitter. *Nearest station* Leighton Buzzard. *Route* Off B488. *Telephone* Leighton Buzzard 3338.

In 1800 the section of the Grand Junction Canal from Braunston to London, via Blisworth, Leighton Buzzard and Tring, was finally opened. That this 95-mile stretch was completed in seven years was due mainly to the brawn of the workmen who dug the 'canal navigations', as they were called, and incidentally gave the word 'navvies' to the English language. It was tough work—and they were tough men who did it. Those were hard-drinking days, in any case, and the canal workers were far from abstemious. More than

The Globe Inn

one astute countryman, on the line of the canal, cashed in on the situation and turned his cottage into a beer-house.

This, in fact, was the origin of The Globe, right by the side of the canal at Linslade. Not that you can see it from the main road, which runs from Leighton Buzzard to Bletchley (B488). A sign on the right about a mile out from Linslade directs one down a steep and rough track, which soon crosses the canal and turns right along the canal bank to The Globe. It is a picturesque old pub, small but full of character. The immediate impression on entering is that the place is run by a family of dwarfs. This illusion is created by the fact that the floor-level behind the bar is some two feet lower than the room itself. It is a relief to find that the row of apparently disembodied heads which greets one really belongs to normal-sized people.

There is only one bar, though in summer, at least, most prefer to drink outside and watch the canal traffic glide by. There is a pleasant garden, and the atmosphere is relaxed in the way which is peculiar to riverside pubs. This is a free house, and at least seven different brews are available.

The canals are coming back into their own once more, and we should drink a toast to the 'navvies' of 1800 who brought the 'Grand Junction'—and The Globe—into being.

128

LITTLE HAMPDEN

The Rising Sun

Free House. Food Snacks. *Special drinks* Benskin's Bitter and mild. *Nearest station* Great Missenden. *Telephone* Hampden Row 393.

Great Hampden and Hampden Row, two or three miles cross-country between Great Missenden and Princes Risborough, have at least two claims to fame. Great Hampden has the Manor, with its memories of 'The Patriot' John Hampden and his cousin Oliver Cromwell. Hampden Row remembers John Masefield, the Poet Laureate, who wrote 'The Everlasting Mercy' whilst living there.

Little Hampden, on the other side of the Missenden road, has no such claim. It is a tiny hamlet, buried far in the beechwoods, and reached by a lane from the main road which ambles gently this way and that, and finally stops with a sigh outside The Rising Sun. There is nowhere left to go.

If ever there was a peaceful spot, this is it. Not only is it restful to the eye, but it is quiet. The tiny church, with its ancient wall-paintings, the old inn gazing across the countryside, seem part of the beechwoods which surround them.

Little has changed in The Rising Sun for generations. No garish lights, no formica-topped counter offend the eye. In winter you drink before an enormous fire, and there are not likely to be many interruptions. In summer most prefer to sit in the pretty garden and gaze across the wooded Buckinghamshire countryside towards Wendover, which from this spot seems almost a bustling city. Everything, of course, is comparative, but if you are looking for a peaceful pub, where a car is almost an intrusion, you will certainly find it at Little Hampden.

LITTLE MARLOW

The King's Head

Brewer Wethered. *Food* Restaurant. *Route* Off A4155. *Nearest station* Marlow or Bourne End. *Telephone* Marlow 4407.

Six hundred years ago there was only one Marlow—and this was it. It is delightful little village, two miles from its newer but bigger brother alon the river, and the same distance from Bourne End.

It is just off the main road, a fairy-tale little place which seems to hav remained unaltered for generations. The familiar pattern is there, churcl manor-house, inn and ancient cottages, compact and self-contained.Th Marlow has no need to be jealous, or sensitive about the addition of th adjective to its name.

The King's Head, a solid Tudor building, was obviously a place of im portance, and still is. Little Marlow was a Royal Manor and was visite by Henry VIII more than once, and in the well-timbered lounge c the inn it takes little imagination to recapture the atmosphere of Tudo times.

There is a delightful rose garden outside, and in the summer months good restaurant is another attraction. The beer is Wethered's, and is from the wood. Despite its great antiquity, The King's Head keeps up to date i its service to customers, and there is an arrangement whereby diners ca: become honorary members of Churchill's and other West End clubs. I! however, the object of your visit is to forget the bright lights this may b achieved by taking a most attractive walk along to the tow-path to Marlow itself. It is only two miles—and you can be back by opening time!

LITTLE MISSENDEN

The Royal Oak

Brewer Aylesbury Brewery Co. *Food* Snacks at bar. *Special drinks* Ind Coope" Bitter and Mild, Draught Guinness, Watney's Red Barrel. *Route* A413 *Nearest station* Great Missenden. *Telephone* Great Missenden 2718.

This is a country pub in every sense, although situated outside the villag on the main Amersham–Great Missenden road. The main road by-passe Little Missenden, and later plays the same trick on Great Missenden. Th Royal Oak, with great acumen, has managed to get the best of both world by being on the main road between the two.

You drive straight off the road into a capacious car-park, with littl danger of being 'boxed-in' if you want to get away quickly—a possibility which is remote!

The Royal Oak has a cosy public-bar, with horse-brasses, harness and other equine trappings of interest to students of nineteenth-century transport. A dart-room adjoins and customers in search of the 'Gents' must beware lest an ear be pinned to the board en route. This would be a serious matter, to say nothing of the delay likely to be caused on the journey.

The saloon-bar, on the left of the entrance, is a particularly good example of intelligent and tasteful modernisation. The room has been enlarged and completely restored, with ample sitting accommodation and exactly the right length of bar—a thing which so often goes wrong when 'improvements' are made to licensed houses. The whole atmosphere of this room is one of mellow charm, with no synthetic 'Old-wordliness'.

The beer consists of Watney's Red Barrel, Ind Coope's Best Bitter and Benskin's Mild. For the connossieur there is draught Guinness, a beer well worth seeking out.

Altogether this is a most pleasant port of call, with a warm welcome every time. Food in quantity is always ready, and whether you spend an evening in The Royal Oak with friends, or just drop in for a quick drink and snack between Aylesbury and London, it is a pub worth noting and remembering.

LITTLE WOOLSTONE

The Barge

Free House. Food Restaurant and snacks. *Special drinks* Flowers' Bitter, Draught Guinness, Home-made wines. *Route* B488. *Nearest station* Bletchley. *Telephone* Milton Keynes 274.

For most of the seven miles from Newport Pagnell to Bletchley the B488 picks its way carefully between the Grand Union Canal on one side and the River Ouzel on the other. At one point the two waterways almost meet, but are kept apart by the village of Little Woolstone—and The Barge.

Like a good many other pubs along the canal it was originally a beer-house supplying the needs of the thirsty navvies working on the cutting. But the thirsty navvies went their way, and so did most of the business at The

Barge. Decrepit and neglected, it eventually became due for demolition until acquired by the present owners, Country Hostelries Ltd.

Once again, the motor-car has been the saviour of another country pub. Restored and improved The Barge today is a very busy place. The fine old building has been given a new lease of life, the interior lovingly restored and a most attractive stone-floored patio added.

Most beer-houses have come a long way since the new licensing regulations made a full licence available to all. One is used to an array of spirits, or sherry and burgundy by the glass, but few are the places where one can call for a glass of home-made birch-sap wine, or take home a bottle of gooseberry. Here, at The Barge, some twenty types of home-made wines are for sale. And let nobody belittle the potency of these delectable brews. Home made they may be, but the recipes our grandmothers used packed a punch and today have been standardised and improved with frightening success.

You can, of course, stick to beer, and drink your Flowers' Bitter or Draught Guinness at the pleasant, copper-topped counter. But if you start with beer it is as well to stick to it, as beer and wine are notorious enemies. However, there is nothing to stop you taking a selection of wines home, and these are on sale in beautifully designed stone bottles especially created for The Barge.

The art of home winemaking is coming back, particularly in the urban areas. A visit to this pub will demonstrate what a worthwhile hobby this is—but keep to the road on the way home. The Grand Union and the Ouze are waiting!

LONG CRENDON

The Churchill Arms

Brewer Aylesbury Brewery Co. *Food* Restaurant and snacks at bar. *Special drinks* Ind Coope's Bitter and Mild, Draught Guinness, Watney's Red Barrel. *Nearest station* Thame. *Telephone* Long Crendon 344.

The county boundary between Thame and Long Crendon twists and turns as it follows the course of the little River Thame for part of its length. The B4011 from Thame to Bletchley crosses the river just outside the town, and once more we are in Buckinghamshire, and two miles further on, in Long Crendon.

The High Street of Long Crendon runs, on the right, from the main road down to the church and the beautiful old Court House, now owned by the National Trust. The Churchill Arms is a picturesque old inn, on the left at the beginning of the High Street. The small lounge is pleasant and cosy, but without much character. This is found more in the larger public-bar, with its gun-racks, high-backed seats, and curious wooden partition vaguely reminiscent of the old box-pews still found in churches in this area. There is a small garden, reached from this bar. This pub belongs to the Aylesbury Brewery Company, and the food supplied is unusual, including such local delicacies as Treacle Tart and Buckinghamshire Bacon Pie.

The district round Long Crendon houses various notabilities, and The Churchill Arms is deservedly a popular rendezvous. It is certainly in keeping with the varied architectural styles which make much of the beauty of this delightful village.

MARLOW

The Bank of England

Brewer Benskin. *Food* Snacks. *Route* B482. *Nearest station* Marlow. *Telephone* Marlow 4203.

At one time there must have been a lot of money made in Marlow, if the names of the pubs are anything to go by. Not only was there The Mint, but also The Royal Exchange and The Bank of England. The first two are gone, the last still with us, but rebuilt and modernised though keeping the old name.

It is about half a mile out of the town, on the Lane End road (B482) and serves a new and large housing estate. The name is not quite unique, though there is said to be only one other pub similarly named in the country, but is still a source of embarrassment to the landlord when answering the 'phone. It is even more of an embarrassment when he takes his annual holiday and books in at an hotel! It is a Benskin house, and was built in 1960 on the site of the older inn. Though small, it has a very cosy and personal atmosphere, and the general décor though perhaps less imaginative than in some modern pubs, at least does not distract one from the beer. There is also a very pleasant little garden.

Being on a main road it has its share of passing trade, though most of the regulars are from the estate. There still seems to be money in Marlow, however, and The Bank of England seems an apt name for a pub which has an annual Club share-out of over £6000. Maybe one should try and become a 'regular' and less of a passer-by.

MARLOW

The Hare & Hounds

Brewer Wethered. *Food* Dining-room. *Special drinks* Good range of wines. *Route* A4155. *Nearest station* Marlow. *Telephone* Marlow 3343.

In 1740 this old and comfortable inn had been standing over two hundred years. Whether business was good or not is debatable, but the fact remains that in that year it was sold as a going concern, together with its 25 acres of hop-fields, for the sum of £50. There is no doubt at all that business is good today. The Hare & Hounds stands on a bend about a mile from Marlow on the Henley road (A4155), a long, low, solid-looking building with that air of having settled into the ground which so many old buildings have.

This is a Wethered house, so even if the beer is not brewed on the premises today, it still doesn't have a long journey to make.

The main bar inside is what one might expect—oak beams, comfortable furniture, and a relaxed atmosphere. Wind and storms may blow outside, but the thick Tudor walls and solid woodwork effectively create a little world within, occupying itself with good cheer and putting the outside world to rights.

Adjoining the main bar is a smaller one, which is also used as a dining-room, and farther on again is a cosy little overflow, ideal for the intimate tête-à-tête. The décor is tasteful and the furniture attractive, the end room exhibiting several modern paintings which blend surprisingly well with the old building. There is virtually no public-bar trade, which is not surprising as the brewers appear to have added this room as an afterthought, making it about the size of a large cupboard, and with as much character.

There is a good car-park to The Hare & Hounds, and a garden. From the direction of Marlow it is easily visible, but coming from Henley you could be round the bend and past it before you can say 'Bitter'. So take it easy—you won't want to miss this.

MARLOW

The Ship WEST STREET

Brewer Wethered. *Food* Tray lunches daily at bar. *Special drinks* Draught Cider. *Route* A4155. *Nearest station* Marlow. *Telephone* Marlow 4360.

Much of the charm of West Street, and indeed of Marlow as a whole, is the enchanting variety of styles in the buildings. The Ship is a good example of sixteenth-century work, with original ship's timbers still visible. Internally it has been modernised with taste, and for a comparatively small inn boasts a surprisingly extensive public-bar. Fish-nets have been used with great ingenuity to decorate this room, and in the small saloon-bar is a good series of old Thames water-colours.

This is a Wethered house, whose brewery is in the town, just round the corner in the High Street. The smallness of the saloon-bar ensures that within minutes you will be talking to somebody, but should you be feeling anti-social there is always the public-bar, where you may play shuv-ha'penny with yourself unmolested. A very good drop of draught cider is to be had here.

MARLOW

The Three Horseshoes BURROUGHS GROVE

Brewer Wethered. *Food* Derbyshire food at bar. *Route* A404. *Nearest station* Marlow. *Telephone* Marlow 3109.

The A404 from High Wycombe to Marlow starts to climb before it leaves the town. By the time it reaches Handy Cross and open country it has climbed nearly 500 feet, and a superb view of the Thames Valley is before you. Dropping down towards Marlow the road divides, a left-hand fork going to Little Marlow, and at the junction is the Three Horseshoes. At least one motor-cyclist, speeding down the long hill from Wycombe, has failed to negotiate the slight bend at this point, and been forced to take a middle course straight through the public-bar window. Whilst this may show a praiseworthy enthusiasm for Wethered's beer, the management prefer a more orthodox entry via the car-park in front, and the door.

This is not a very ancient building, but it is a homely one. Both public and saloon-bars are small and cosy, and the friendly atmosphere tends to make the casual passer-by stay just that bit longer. There is no keg beer, the draught is all from the wood and is Wethered's Best Bitter and Ordinary Bitter.

MARLOW

The Two Brewers   ST PETER STREET

Brewer Wethered. *Bedrooms* 3. *Food* Snacks at bar. *Nearest station* Marlow. *Telephone* Marlow 4140

The High Street of Marlow branches left from the High Wycombe to Henley road in the centre of the town. It runs down to the river, ending at the Parish Church and the famous suspension bridge built by Tierney Clarke in 1831. Both are interesting, but much of Marlow's charm lies in the quiet side-streets, with their dignified Georgian buildings and sudden glimpses of the river.

Such a street is St Peter Street, running parallel to the High Street and ending on the river bank. Almost on the river is The Two Brewers, an old and picturesque pub, which in its time has seen more Marlow traffic than might be thought. The ancient black beams and low ceilings have sheltered many a traveller from across the river, for this road led, in former days to the old wooden bridge displaced by Clarke's masterpiece. A few feet from the door of The Two Brewers is a little wharf, giving a most attractive view of the Berkshire bank, the weir, and the bridge.

The present building dates from 1686, and in one room may be seen a picture of the old bridge in its heyday. It is a restful spot, away from the

136

The Two Brewers

bustle of traffic, where one can relax in comfort. The beer is Wethered's, and the food is good. Small wonder Jerome K. Jerome chose to stay there while writing *Three Men in a Boat*.

MARSH GIBBON

The Plough

Brewer Morrell. *Food* Snacks. *Special drinks* 'Varsity' Keg, Draught Guinness. *Nearest station* Bicester. *Telephone* Stratton Audley 305.

The charm of many English villages lies in the grouping of the most important buildings, and in their relationship to each other. Here, at Marsh Gibbon, the church stands a little way up a lane, whilst The Plough looks up the lane from the village street. Between them sprawls the rambling Elizabethan manor-house, with its adjoining farm buildings, successfully bridging the gap between the temporal and the spiritual.

The Plough was at one time a coaching-inn, though the familiar arched entrance and courtyard are no longer there. The two bars are very different in style, and, as so often happens in rural inns, the public-bar seems to be almost more important than the saloon. This public-bar, anyway, has been effectively modernised and is a far cry from the 'spit-and-sawdust' so often found in towns. The dart-board is there, of course, but perfectly lit and positioned. The bar is bright, the fittings efficiently arranged, and the colour-scheme attractive.

The saloon-lounge is smaller, and more in character with the age of this house. There are some fine old beams, interspersed with a few newer ones, and the atmosphere of an old pub is happily retained. Between these two rooms is sort of a lobby, possibly the original entrance, with an enormous ingle-nook. Not so happily this has been decorated with of all things, wall-paper with a design of bricks! No doubt, in time, the beams will be covered with paper designed to look like old oak!

But this is a minor criticism, and would not be worth mentioning had not the remainder of the decoration been carried out with such good effect.

There is an attractive garden for customers, and this includes swings and a see-saw for the children. Not many pubs are as thoughtful as this, and The Plough underlines its concern for the younger generation by also providing a special 'Children's Room', with small seats and tables.

Marsh Gibbon lies about two miles north of the Aylesbury–Banbury road (A41) and is just in Buckinghamshire. It is a Morrell house, and these Oxford brewers point out that it is their only pub in this county. Draught Guinness is among the beers provided, and, needless to say 'tots' are served.

MARSWORTH

The White Lion

Free House. Food Separate snack-bar. *Special drinks* Younger's and Flowers' Bitter, Whitbread's Tankard, Flowers' Keg. *Nearest station* Tring. *Telephone* Tring 2325.

Marsworth is a tiny village on the Grand Union Canal, about two miles north of Tring. It is an odd sort of area, this, flat and open, though the views are limited by the long, sloping banks of the reservoirs belonging to the Canal Company.

The White Lion, on the road to Ivinghoe and its beacon, lies next to the wicked little hump-back bridge over the canal. It is a small pub, at an awkward spot on a narrow road, and it is therefore just as well that there is a good car-park in the field opposite.

The little public-bar at the front is often crowded, though there is plenty of room in the lounge and saloon-bar behind. In the summer the gardens, along by the canal, are extremely popular, with the bare, round outline of Ivinghoe Beacon to the north dominating the scene.

Steps lead down to the canal-bank, just by the bridge, giving an added touch of the picturesque to this interesting pub.

This is an area for the bird-watcher, for the immense reservoirs attract

The White Lion

hundreds of migratory birds, some of which are rarely seen anywhere else in England. It is obvious that with this wealth of natural resources there is plenty to entertain the visitor. It might be the canal, it might be the reservoir. But the most popular pastime of all is waiting for two motorists to decide to cross the hump-back bridge at once. That, and bird-watching from the bar.

MEDMENHAM

The Dog & Badger

Brewer Wethered. *Bedrooms* 3. *Food* Restaurant. *Route* A4155. *Nearest station* Marlow. *Telephone* Hambledon 362.

Few would imagine, as they wander round this peaceful Thames-side village, that the events of twenty years made this place famous in the annals of evil and debauchery. But that is human nature. The fact that at the time of the Dissolution of the Monasteries the Abbey was described as housing only two monks, whose assets were 'Movable goods £1 : 3 : 8d; Woods none: Debts none:' is quite overshadowed by the scandalous events which took place from 1745 onwards. Not that The Dog & Badger had very much to do with these goings-on. On the contrary, this fifteenth-century inn, with its three dormer windows and ancient woodwork, seems to have been honoured, in that banns for weddings had to be published here before being read in church.

This is another Wethered house, on the main road between Marlow and Henley (A4155), and close to the river. You come to it suddenly, the road twisting sharply as it goes through the little village. Near The Dog & Badger a quiet lane leads down to the river-bank and the site of the old ferry where King Charles crossed in 1678. On the same side of the main road is the ruin of the old Cistercian monastery beside the river. This was the head-quarters of the notorious 'Hellfire Club' founded in 1745 by Sir Francis Dashwood of West Wycombe. Black Magic, and sexual orgies of all kinds were carried on here, and at the famous West Wycombe Caves, and although most of the evidence has been destroyed, the tales linger on. Eighteenth-century historians, of undoubted reliability, describe the statues with pornographic inscriptions, the indecent church-paintings and the door in the shape of a female vagina. All these, understandably, are no more. But The Dog & Badger, even more understandably, is still with us.

MONK'S RISBOROUGH

The Nag's Head

Brewer Benskin. *Food* Snacks. *Route* A4010. *Nearest station* Princes Risborough. *Telephone* Princes Risborough 2941.

This charming little Benskin house lies just off the main road at Monk's Risborough, less than a mile from the more famous Princes Risborough.

Some landlords have been known to deplore the straightening and widening of main roads, but here the old road has been left, running right by The Nag's Head, and providing a convenient car-park for callers. It is a neat and tidy place, white-walled with gay window-boxes and hanging flower-baskets, with a pretty post-and-chain fence around.

Inside, it is small and snug. It does not give an impression of great age, although it is old enough, nor has it tried to be 'with it' by means of trick lighting or fancy ironwork. The result is eminently satisfying, and few pubs are entirely this.

PENN

The Crown

Free House. Food Restaurant and snacks at bar. *Special drinks* Draught Bass, Whitbread's Tankard, Wines. *Route* B474. *Nearest station* Beaconsfield. *Telephone* Penn 3184.

Some three miles north-west of Beaconsfield, on the B474 to Hazlemere, the little village of Penn looks out across the rolling beechwoods. Unlike most villages, where the church is usually the centre, Penn has its church on the edge, practically the first building met on the way from Beaconsfield.

The Crown

The Crown is a handsome, gabled, brick building almost opposite the church. It is of solid Elizabethan construction, with stone-flagged floors and massive chimneys.

Inside is the picturesque and cosy 'XVIth-century Bar' and the more modern restaurant bar. The old bar was at one time a coffin-maker's shop, when The Crown was divided into several properties, as was the custom. This was not the only undertaking on the premises. An old barn at the rear was a wheel-wright's workshop at one time, and is now used as an 'overflow' bar at week-ends and in the summer. Many of the original wheel-wright's tools hang on the walls, reminding us of the high standard of skill required for this ancient and important calling.

It is not in every village inn that we are fortunate enough to meet 'The Intellect and Valour of Britain' on the way to the toilets. At The Crown we do—or at least we pass a large Victorian engraving which makes this bold claim, and depicts, on the crowded canvas, a cross-section of the famous ones of the day. It is a sobering experience.

The Crown is a free house, dealing in Whitbread's Tankard, Red Barrel and Draught Bass, and is owned by Finchs.

PENN STREET, near Amersham

The Hit or Miss

Brewer Wethered. *Food* Snacks at bar. *Special drinks* Vintage Cider. *Nearest station* Beaconsfield or Amersham. *Telephone* Holmer Green 3109.

The village of Penn Street, just south of the Amersham–High Wycombe road (A404) would not, at first sight, be classified as an industrial centre. But this is the Chilterns, and the Chilterns means wood-working. The days of the wood-bodger, working alone in the beechwoods turning chair-legs on a pole-lathe, are gone. The industry is today highly organised, and Penn Street village includes the modern factory of Messrs. Dancer & Hearne, whose chairs are found in every corner of the country. The firm also owns one of the two village inns. This is The Hit or Miss, a long and low building, on the road near the factory. There is a public-bar on the left, and three saloon-bars on the right. As befits a pub so closely connected with the trade, the interior decorations are unusual, in that they show various aspects of chair-making. The brasses are not the usual ones. Here they show types of chairs, whilst on a wall are samples of the various kinds of wood used in the trade. Several wood-working tools are on display. Not that The Hit or Miss is by any means a museum. The ancient beams and timbers are eminently suitable for the décor, which is not too obtrusive. The beer is Wethered's of Marlow, and has been since 1798. The chairs, needless to say, are Dancer & Hearne's.

PRINCES RISBOROUGH

The Pink & Lily   PARSLOW'S HILLOCK

Brewer Benskin. *Bedrooms* 2. *Food* Snacks. *Special drinks* Watney's Red Barrel. *Nearest station* Princes Risborough. *Telephone* Hampden Row 308.

> *Never there came to the Pink*
> *Two such men as we think.*
> *Never came there to the Lily*
> *Two men quite so richly silly*

Like others in this book, this isolated pub between Lacey Green and Prince Risborough has literary associations. Though impossible to find in any collection of his poems, the lines above were written by Rupert Brooke, and a copy of the full poem hangs in one of the rooms. Rupert Brooke stayed here often before the Great War, exploring the Chilterns with his friends by day and amusing himself by writing doggerel in the pub in the evenings.

At least two other things make The Pink & Lily an unusual pub. There is no bar, just a serving-hatch. Customers stand around in the passage, or sink into one of the comfortable chairs in the adjoining two rooms. It is also the home of an ancient game called 'Ringing the Bull' in which players try to swing a copper bull-ring on a piece of string on to a hook.

This is a Benskin house, providing bitter and mild from the wood with Red Barrel from the keg. Yet another oddity in this unusual pub is that the landlord has to go down into his very fine cellar to draw every pint. He doesn't mind, so why should you?

PRINCES RISBOROUGH

The Three Horseshoes

Free House. Food Snacks. *Special drinks* Worthington E, Younger's and Benskin's Bitter, Whitbread's Tankard. *Nearest station* Princes Risborough. *Telephone* Princes Risborough 737.

To describe this picturesque old pub as in Princes Risborough is, perhaps, a little misleading. It is about two miles from the centre of Risborough, down a lane which, after crossing the railway by way of a frightening zigzag bridge, eventually leads to Saunderton. But the lane, and the bridge, are worth negotiating to find The Three Horseshoes, for here is another country pub which has been made comfortable and attractive in a way our ancestors never knew.

An odd sort of lobby has been built on to the front of the original building, perhaps as a sort of parking-place for small fry who might otherwise spend the time in the car blowing the horn and letting off the hand-brake. The same sort of arrangement is seen at The Brickmaker's Arms on Wheeler End Common, and indeed this free house is under the same ownership, which probably accounts for it.

Most people come to it from a distance, the result being a friendly atmosphere and a complete absence of that feeling of being an intruder which is so often present when visiting a real 'local'.

There is a pleasant garden, if the kids can't be trusted in the lobby, or are likely to ruin your drink by making faces at you through the glass!

The beer, by the way, is draught Benskin's and Younger's bitters, and Worthington E and Whitbread's Tankard from the keg.

QUAINTON

The Sportsman

Brewer Aylesbury Brewery Co. *Food* Snacks. *Special drinks* Ind Coope's Bitter, Draught Guinness, Watney's Red Barrel, Benskin's Mild. *Nearest station* Quainton. *Telephone* Quainton 257.

Almost opposite the gates of Waddesdon Manor, that French baronial pile of the Rothschilds, the road to Quainton branches off the A41 and heads north into the hinterland of Buckinghamshire. By no stretch of the imagination could this be called a densely populated area and when, after some three miles, Quainton is reached, the sense of arrival is very real.

Here, in this remote village, little has changed through the years. And this is as it should be. For it was here in 1773 that Thomas Lipscombe was born, destined to be the great historian of Buckinghamshire, devoting his life to collecting information and the recording of the history of his beloved county. It cannot have changed a great deal since his day.

The village green, criss-crossed by paths and surrounded by tiny cottages, slopes gently upwards to the ancient market-cross. At the bottom end, just round the corner, The Sportsman snoozes under its massive layer of thatch, as if nothing could ever wake it. And probably nothing ever will. The sturdy beams and timbers have watched generations of village children grow up and become old. The two tiny bars have echoed to the sound of laughter for nearly four hundred years, and have been the clearing-house for village gossip for as long.

There is nothing modern about The Sportsman. It is as a village pub ought to be, complete with ingle-nook fireplace, horse-brasses and

yellow-plastered walls. The Aylesbury Brewery Company own it. Let us
hope they never change it, or Thomas Lipscombe would most surely turn
in his grave.

SEER GREEN, near Beaconsfield

The Jolly Cricketers

Brewer Wethered. *Food* Snacks. *Nearest station* Beaconsfield. *Telephone*
Jordans 3108.

The village of Seer Green lies roughly midway between Beaconsfield, on
the A40, and Chalfont St Giles on the A413. It is not a particularly picturesque village, and does not seem to worry about it. A mile away is
Jordans, with the Mayflower Barn and the humble graves of William Penn
and his family. That, perhaps, is the reason why Seer Green prefers to be
unobtrusive and to get on with its daily business undisturbed.

The Jolly Cricketers, one of the two village pubs, shows the same self-
effacement. It is old, as most Chiltern pubs are, and has been run by the
same family for nearly a hundred years. It is clean and cosy, but the hand
of the 'restorer' has not so far touched it to any extent. The brown woodwork and yellow plaster are at least genuine. There is no pretence at
modernising—no fairy-lamps round the bar. But the beer (Wethered's) is
well kept, which to many is more important than doubtful Elizabethan
timbers and recently installed ingle-nooks.

The Jolly Cricketers has three large and comfortable rooms, all served from
the one, long, central bar. The customers are mainly local, and village matters
are debated with an intensity of feeling that is almost frightening. But no
heads get broken, and everybody trots peacefully home. This may be due to
the ancient board displayed in the central room carrying the good advice:

> *'Call frequently*
> *Drink moderately,*
> *Pay honourably,*
> *Be of Good Company,*
> *Part friendly,*
> *Go home quietly.'*

Here, at least, you know where you are—in a village pub with no pretentions to being anything else.

SLOUGH

The Jolly Londoner
BRITWELL ESTATE

Brewer Watney. *Food* Snacks. *Nearest station* Slough. *Telephone* Slough 29536.

Slough has seen a great deal of development in latter years, with large housing estates spreading into what was the countryside only a short time ago. Mostly these estates are well planned, with shopping precincts, churches and car-parks as an automatic part of the development. There also has to be a pub, which in a large estate like this one soon becomes a very definite social centre.

The Britwell Estate is to the west of Slough, just north of the famous Trading Estate. Most of the residents are Londoners, and it was a pleasant thought to give their 'local' the appropriate name of The 'Jolly Londoner'. (The name was chosen after a competition by Watney's, whose house it is, and was won by a staunch teetotaller!)

Built in 1962, it is a very good example of modern pub design and décor, with a character all of its own. There is a large public-bar, and two smaller saloon-bars, in one of which, at week-ends, music is provided. There is little passing trade on this estate, and the atmosphere is that of a real 'local'. Being Londoners, and jolly ones at that, the customers themselves take part in the entertainment. And not only the young ones. Young Bert may rattle the glasses with the latest beat number, but this won't stop Dad from getting up and quavering through 'Roses of Picardy' with the entire pub joining in the chorus.

The Britwell Community Centre is just along the road, but I doubt if it is as jolly as 'The Londoner'.

SPEEN

The Old Plow

Free House. Bedrooms 3. *Food* Restaurant. *Special drinks* Worthington E, Flowers' Keg and Draught Bitter. *Nearest station* Princes Risborough. *Telephone* Hampden Row 300.

Three miles north of High Wycombe the Great Missenden road turns abruptly right up Cryer's Hill. The road straight ahead, however, probes deep into the Chiltern countryside and eventually reaches Speen, a straggling little village at the top of a hill. Past the cross-roads the road suddenly plunges wildly down, negotiating a hair-pin bend of almost Alpine severity to reach the floor of the valley—and The Old Plow.

This beautifully sited seventeenth-century inn has been famous for a very long time. True, it was kept for some years by Ishbel MacDonald, daughter of the politician, but in its very early days was mentioned with approval by no less a critic than Samuel Pepys.

Pepys has gone, and Ishbel has retired to her native heath. The Old Plow continues its tradition of good drink and good food, and the visitors to it are many.

It is not a large building, and at week-ends the visitor may well find himself pinned against one of the many massive pillars which support the low ceilings. The bar counter is adequate under normal conditions, but at times of stress may become as inaccessible as the Himalayas. With any luck the congestion will be eased by occasional migrations to the restaurant—a lovely room and much more comfortable than the bar, particularly at week-ends.

The answer, of course, is to visit The Old Plow during the week. Then one can appreciate the beauties of this fine old pub at leisure. Then one can drink one's Youngers' or Flowers' beer (for this is a free house) in comfort without finding that your next-door neighbour has guzzled half of it by mistake. And if things are unusually quiet the licensee may tell you of his efforts to piece together the history of The Plow—for though one has no wish to tarnish the memory of Ishbel and her father, no doubt the place has housed many equally interesting characters since it first opened its doors in 1610.

STOKE POGES

The Dog & Pot   ROGERS LANE

Brewer Courage. *Food* Snacks at bar. *Nearest station* Slough. *Telephone* Farnham Common 175.

The Stoke Poges of Thomas Gray, despite the gradual approach of Slough, still remains a separate entity and still retains a certain rural charm. Rogers Lane, just west of the Slough–Gerrards Cross road (A332) is a later development of the old village, and runs roughly parallel to the main road.

The Dog & Pot serves this newer part of the village, and is a mecca for the military-minded. In both the public- and saloon-bars the walls are covered with regimental badges of every kind, handsomely mounted and shining brightly. Swords abound, plumes wave in the breeze, and there is a wonderful selection of silver tankards, each bearing a regimental crest.

It is great fun trying to identify your own particular badge, and accounts for the odd sight of earnest drinkers commuting from saloon to public and back again whilst engaged in their search.

However, despite the military appearance of The Dog & Pot, the natives are friendly and unlikely to cause trouble. The brew, it is hardly necessary to add, is Courage's.

STONY STRATFORD

The Plough

Brewer Charles Webb Ltd. *Bedrooms* 3. *Food* Restaurant and snacks. *Special drinks* Draught Guinness, 'Noggin' Keg. *Route* A5. *Nearest station* Bletchley. *Telephone* Stony Stratford 2276.

Stony Stratford straddles the A5 London–Holyhead trunk road just before it leaves Buckinghamshire and enters Northamptonshire. The Plough is at the cross-roads in the centre of the town—a busy spot despite the advent of the M1 farther north. It is a large Victorian building, its two capacious bars rarely idle, and has that cheerful atmosphere so typical of the main-road pub whose customers are ever-changing as they break their journey for 'a quick one' en route.

Externally there seems at first sight to be something odd about the building. Part of it seems to have a most un-pub-like design, and though the architecture is choice Victorian, the tall, narrow windows and grey stone are more in keeping with a church school or chapel. This part is the public-bar, and until 1935 it was, in fact, the local elementary school. Built in 1873 it was later acquired by the brewers, Charles Webb Ltd., and incorporated into the main structure when The Plough began to burst at the seams.

The original part of the pub was then given over to the saloon-bar, and accounts for its size. But even here there is more than a tinge of Victoriana, and the door to the street contains some handsome stained glass.

Probably little of this is noticed by the hurrying traveller—and the locals take it for granted. All the same it is something unusual, and John Betjeman would certainly feel at home in the public-bar.

SWAN BOTTOM

The Gate

Free House. Food Snacks. *Special drinks* Worthington E, Draught Guinness, Younger's Scotch Ale. *Nearest station* Great Missenden. *Telephone* The Lee 368.

Out-of-the-ordinary pubs are hard to find—in more than one sense. Swan Bottom is a cross-roads on the winding country lane which starts at Chesham, widens out through Chartridge, finally joining the Wendover–Missenden road at a point almost opposite the Dunsmore turn a mile-and-a-half from Wendover. The Gate stands alone, some two miles from the main road.

It is a free house, and very, very old. On first sight it does not give an appearance of great age. The eye is taken rather by the impressive avenue of limes leading from the car-park to the inn door—an unusual enough introduction to an unusual pub. A great deal has been done to The Gate since the days when it was a ploughman's cottage. Ceilings have come down, walls demolished and floors levelled, yet with all that there is no sense of 'tarting-up'. It remains a modest pub, and in common with many another country inn, the public-bar is obviously the social centre.

The alterations to the building brought to light several odd items of bygone days. There are some hand-made bottles from a firm in High Wycombe, round and bulbous and almost impossible to stand up on end. The familiar 'yard of ale' made of glass is hanging up, but this one is an oddity in being made of red glass.

But the most intriguing fact about The Gate is the story that somewhere

150

on the premises is buried a bucketful of gold coins. Not even the most diligent search on the part of the landlord during renovations revealed this treasure, and no customer has ever laid claim to it.

Still, there is always a chance, and there is still plenty to see. But don't let the licensee catch you digging up the bar floor with a pick—he is rather good at using one himself!

TURVILLE

The Bull & Butcher

Brewer Henley Brewery Co. *Food* Snacks at bar—separate dining annexe. *Nearest station* High Wycombe. *Telephone* Turville Heath 283.

Turville is a lovely village—the loveliest in the county, some say. Snug and secluded, it lies tucked away in a fold of the leafy hills to the west of Lane End. All the elements are there to make it the sort of village to dream about.

The Bull & Butcher

There is the tiny village green with the squat-towered church behind, a row of ancient dormered cottages another side, a farm and The Bull & Butcher to complete the picture. All around it the wooded slopes of the Chilterns rise gently to form a perfect framework for this rural scene.

As might be expected The Bull & Butcher is a half-timbered building of Tudor origin, with a massive chimney-stack characteristic of the period. The ceilings are low, the floors uneven, giving great charm to the place. Most of the ground floor is taken up by the two bars, but the saloon-lounge, on the right, has a quaint little annexe for diners. The Bull & Butcher is proud of its food, but very wisely does not let this intrude in the important matter of drinking at the bar.

The Henley Brewery Company own The Bull & Butcher, and acquired it after it had been sadly neglected for many years.

Nobody knows how long it has been there or how old the licence is. But the church, across the green, appears to keep a fatherly eye on it, and seems to approve. The only thing that comes between them is the red bus from High Wycombe, which ends its run here and, understandably, seems disinclined to start on the return journey. In a setting such as this the bus looks as incongruous as a visitor from Mars. Should the day arrive when Martians *do* visit Turville let us hope The Bull & Butcher will not have altered its looks, though the low beams of the ceiling may have to be adapted slightly for pointed heads!

WADDESDON

The Crooked Billet

Brewer Aylesbury Brewery Co. *Food* Restaurant at rear, snacks at bar. *Special drinks* Ind Coope's Bitter and Mild, Draught Guinness, Watney's Red Barrel. *Route* A41. *Nearest station* Aylesbury. *Telephone* Crendon Underwood 239.

This attractive old inn is a favourite stopping-place for the motorist on the Aylesbury–Bicester road (A41). It lies at Kingswood about three miles from Waddesdon, on the Bicester side, with a good car-park and petrol-station adjoining.

The Crooked Billet

It looks like an old inn, with its three dormer windows and low stone walling, and has a quaint sign swinging by the roadside, which is worth reading. The interior is even older, with that cosy and welcoming atmosphere produced by the combination of old beams, solid furniture and shining brass ornaments.

There is plenty of room in both saloon- and public-bars for the ever-changing clientèle, for like most main-road inns it may be full to capacity one minute and quiet the next. Situated in an agricultural area, with few houses near, it does a steady business with the local farming fraternity. And in the Vale of Aylesbury farming is very 'steady'—and certainly good 'business'. The old stables at the back have been converted into a restaurant —the 'Saddle-Room'—which is open every lunch-time from 12.30 until 2 p.m. This is an Aylesbury Brewery Company inn with Benskin's, Watney's and Ind Coope's beers on tap.

One word of warning. The main bar was once two separate cottages. The dividing-wall has been removed, but the two front-doors remain, side-by-side. This is not apparent on entering, however. It is on turning to leave that the sudden apparition of a double-door ahead causes strong men to blanch and reach for the Alka-Seltzer. But all is well—just remember to make for the left-hand one.

WENDOVER

The King & Queen

Brewer Ind Coope. *Food* Snacks. *Special drinks* Benskin's Bitter and Mild, Watney's Red Barrel. *Route* A413. *Nearest station* Wendover. *Telephone* Wendover 3272.

The fact that The King & Queen stands right on the main road from Amersham and is practically the first building you meet in Wendover is a mixed blessing for this pub. The traveller in the opposite direction, having weaved his way through the bends of this little village, is tempted to put his foot down on the straight and speed towards Great Missenden, missing the swinging sign of this interesting house. This would be a pity. The King & Queen is old, dating from the time of Henry VIII, and has heard the tramp of Cromwell's troops through the town on at least one occasion. The old beams are still there, gazing down approvingly at the bright bar and comfortable high-backed seats. It comes as rather a surprise to notice the decorations. Malayan knives, carved wood replicas of firearms, an ancient clock and a signed photograph of The Crazy Gang adorn the walls. But it all fits in, and nothing seems incongruous, such is the charm of old inns which move with the times, yet keep their character.

This is an Ind Coope house, so Benskin's Mild and Bitter and Watney's Red Barrel are available, in the confusing fashion of brewery groups today. But at least there is no confusion when you visit the toilets. One door is labelled 'Kings', the other 'Queens'. Perhaps this is something to do with The Crazy Gang. Henry VIII would certainly have appreciated them.

WENDOVER

The Shoulder of Mutton

Brewer Wethered. *Bedrooms* 6. *Food* Restaurant and snacks at bar. *Route* B4010. *Nearest station* Wendover. *Telephone* Wendover 3223.

Some pubs are for the old, some for the middle-aged, and some for the young. This one, just by the station in Wendover, is definitely for the young.

154

The names of the bars give an indication of their characteristics, the only one with a normal label being the 'Public'. There is 'The Snug', 'The Beefeater Bar' and 'The Softbeat Bar'. Despite its name you can drink, amongst other things, Wethered's Best Bitter or Mild in 'The Beefeater' while looking down to 'The Softbeat Bar' below where couples dance or sit in tactfully subdued lighting. This happens on Thursdays, Fridays and Saturdays.

The youthful clientèle is composed largely of R.A.F. apprentices from near-by Halton Camp thankfully spreading their wings.

It is a pleasant sight, and if you are over thirty makes you wish you were not.

WEST WYCOMBE

The George & Dragon

Brewer Simonds. *Bedrooms* 4. *Food* Restaurant and snacks at bar. Whitebait and steaks a speciality. *Route* A40. *Nearest station* High Wycombe. *Telephone* High Wycombe 202.

This attractive old inn is situated in the middle of the National Trust village of West Wycombe, on the A40 to Oxford. There is plenty of history in the village, from West Wycombe church with its extraordinary golden ball, perched on top of the hill, to the Dashwood mausoleum just below, and the Hellfire Caves cut into the hill, home of the notorious eighteenth-century Hellfire Club. The George & Dragon is older than all of these, and for nearly five hundred years has been a focal point of village life.

It was renovated in 1720, being given the standard treatment of a flat brick front. From the attractive cobbled courtyard at the rear the solid old ships' timbers of the original building may still be seen. The massive and colourful oval lead sign, showing St George doing battle with the dragon, was almost certainly part of the 1720 improvement.

Another pleasant feature of this old inn is the family of white fantail pigeons who live in the loft above the stables. These were introduced when The George & Dragon was a coaching-inn, and were used to carry messages to Oxford and Acton giving news of coach departures. Internally there is no doubt that this is a very old building indeed. The different floor-levels confirm this, and indeed hide a 'priest's-hole' between two upstairs rooms. Not unexpectedly there are legendary associations with the Hellfire Club. A secret tunnel is thought to run from the inn to the caves, and the ghostly figure of a white nun has been seen in the garden.

On a more mundane level good food and snacks are provided for the present-day traveller, and the beer is Simonds.

WEXHAM

The Red Lion STOKE GREEN

Free House. Food Snacks and lunches 12.30/1.45. *Special drinks* Simonds' and Whitbread's Draught Beers, Whitbread's Tankard. *Nearest station* Slough. *Telephone* Slough 21739.

Few pubs have quite the character of The Red Lion. Externally it seems normal enough, set well back from the road with a pleasant green in front and a semicircular drive sweeping up to the front door and away again.

But once inside that front door you realise you are in a pub very different from most. The stone flags lead to an enormously high counter from which the landlord peers down at you, examining the top of your head with interest. To the right is a room devoted to darts and other games, and by the door is an ancient piano. Immediately opposite the bar is a tiny little room with a bench each side and a table between, the whole thing not more than six feet wide and enclosed by a little half-door exactly like a box-pew in a church. A great curved wooden wall, undoubtedly of seventeenth-century construction, encloses yet another small room. All these places form part of the public-bar. The saloon-bar is along a passage, up some steps, and is revealed as one more tiny room with a counter about three feet long for serving. From the stone flags below to the yellowing and aged plaster of the ceiling The Red Lion proclaims its independence—and the fact that it is a free house. Here there is no need for phoney gimmicks or brash brassware. The Red Lion is old, and you take it as you find it.

Upstairs are rooms used for functions, and The Red Lion has had a long association with the Stoke Green Cricket Club founded in 1836, which meets there. Not often is the personality of a pub quite so marked. Your first visit will certainly be the fore-runner of many, for nobody quite believes it the first time!

WHEELER END

The Brickmaker's Arms

Free House. Food Snacks at bar and at tables. *Special drinks* Worthington E, Draught Bass, Younger's Bitter, Benskin's Mild, Flowers' Keg, Watney's Red Barrel. *Nearest station* High Wycombe. *Telephone* Lane End 526.
Though progress and development have come to many parts of Buckinghamshire, the old customs and traditions die hard. Pockets of resistance seem to have established themselves against the encircling hordes, and here, high up on Wheeler End Common, the old crafts were carried on until the end. The last of the chair-bodgers plied his trade round here. The last survivors of the local band of Mummers performed in The Brickmaker's Arms until 1933, and the fast-disappearing genuine Buckinghamshire dialect still finds

The Brickmaker's Arms

a stronghold in the little cottages which surround the as yet untamed common.

But now The Brickmaker's, for so long a rural retreat, has become conscious of its age and the importance of its position. It lies across country between the A40 and the Marlow–Stokenchurch roads and is enormously popular with High Wycombe folk for whom it is an easy journey.

But the character of the place has been kept, even if it has been altered out of all recognition. It is pleasant and mellow, and good furnishings and carpets, careful lighting and efficient service still leave room for one to appreciate its age. It is a skilful mixture of old and new, and carries it off with the dignity of an old lady who does not resent the present age, even if she does not really approve of it.

It is a free house, with a bewildering selection of drinks and an equally bewildering collection of toby-mugs and tankards on the walls.

Maybe The Brickmaker's is a little self-conscious these days, and, for an old lady, has just a shade too much make-up. But at least they did take out the electric organ.

WHITCHURCH

The White Swan

Brewer Aylesbury Brewery Co. *Food* Snacks. *Special drinks* Ind Coope's Bitter and Mild, Draught Guinness, Watney's Red Barrel. *Route* A413. *Nearest station* Aylesbury. *Telephone* Whitchurch 228.

Of the three main roads which meet in the centre of Aylesbury before continuing on their diverse ways, perhaps the A413 to Buckingham is the most pleasant. Certainly it carries the least traffic and gives the motorist opportunity to admire the rolling landscape and the distant views this part of Buckinghamshire affords.

Four miles along this road at the top of a hill is the village of Whitchurch. The White Swan, on the right at the beginning of the village, is only one of the many picturesque buildings which line the village street and display to the discerning the many styles of English architecture.

158

This is hunting country, and The White Swan is closely connected with hunting, show-jumping and, in fact, equestrian achievement of every kind. It is of venerable age, and at one time the inn, with its stables and numerous outhouses, had a thatched roof of truly noble proportions.

But in 1959 a disastrous fire destroyed the thatch and a good deal of the structure. The restoration of the inn after the fire was carried out with such skill that nowhere in the building can one distinguish the original from the restored. The saloon-lounge, with its little bar, cosy alcoves and sporting prints seems to have remained intact for generations. The talk is of horses and of hunting, at any time of the year. This is not surprising as the licensee is related to Dorian Williams, who probably knows more about horses than any man alive.

But the real surprise of The White Swan is found outside, in the attractive garden. Here we find one of the most extensive aviaries for miles around, created and maintained for the benefit of the customers. Golden Pheasants are there, quail and duck sit around with ever-watchful eye, and the homely budgerigar hungrily attacks its spray of millet. At night the aviary is lit, and what a delightful spot it is. The Aylesbury Brewery Company should be proud of The White Swan—and it makes a change from horses!

WINSLOW

The Bell

Free House. Special drinks Younger's Bitter. *Route* A413. *Nearest station* Aylesbury. *Telephone* Winslow 141.

The late-lamented Sam Goldwyn once remarked 'There is no such thing as bad publicity.' One could go a stage further and say that there is no such thing as no publicity, for extreme self-effacement and determination not to publicise can rebound on itself and become almost a gimmick.

The Bell at Winslow stands in a striking position in the Market Square, looking straight up the Buckingham road. It is a large and handsome structure dominating the surrounding buildings and was obviously at one time a posting-house of some importance. Today, at first sight, it appears to be closed. The front door is unyielding, the curtains drawn, and there is nothing to indicate that there is life within. But this is a pub with a difference. This is an inn for the connoisseur.

The old arch at the side provides the answer. A door under this leads into a passage, past a little office so Dickensian in atmosphere that one feels that Bob Cratchit has only just that minute slipped out, past several locked doors, until the murmur of voices is heard. A flight of stairs leads to the dark unknown above—another passage probes the more remote corners of the rambling building.

The voices come from a room used as the bar. Here the landlord sits at his table (there is no counter) and dispenses drinks from a massive mahogany sideboard. At the side the handles of an ancient beer-engine mark the fountain-head of Younger's Bitter, drawing it up from the deep cellar below.

The customers are local, the talk is local. The same family has run the pub since 1814, and if you are lucky you will be shown ancient account-books and ledgers which are fascinating but depressing! Whiskey at 16/6d. a gallon and sherry at 18/6d. tend to make one sigh for happier days—until the wages book is produced!

Until 1914 The Bell brewed its own beer on the premises, refusing to be tied to any commercial brewery. Today it retains its independence by remaining a free house and selling the beer it chooses. It is a pub for those interested in the past, for those who prefer to sip their beer and gaze into the fire, and who feel at one with the company and the talk of country things.

There are many pubs in Buckinghamshire, but not another like this.

INDEXES

Index of Pubs

Index to Brewers

AYLESBURY BREWERY COMPANY

BENSKIN

CHARRINGTON

COURAGE

FLOWERS

FREE HOUSES

FRIARY MEUX

HARMAN

HENLEY BREWERY COMPANY

HOOK NORTON BREWERY

HUNT EDMUNDS

IND COOPE

MORLAND

Index to Special Draught Beers, etc.

Supplied by brewers other than those to which the house is 'tied'—or in Free Houses.

Bass, Draught

Benskin's Bitter

Benskin's Mild

Brakspear's Henley Pale Ale

Draught Cider

170

Courage E.I.P.A.

Aston Rowant, Lambert Arms, 11

Double Diamond

Banbury, The Inn Within, 13
Chipping Norton, The Fox, 23
Hartwell, Bugle Horn, 117
Minster Lovell, Old Swan, 40

Oxford, Forte's Motor Lodge, 43
   Golden Cross, 44, 45
   Turl Tavern, 49
Tetsworth, The Swan, 59

Flowers Bitter

Bledlow, Red Lions, 84
Forty Green, Royal Standard of
   England, 110
Kingham, Langston Arms, 37
Linslade, The Globe, 127, 128

Little Woolstone, The Barge, 131
Marsworth, White Lion, 138, 139
Russell's Water, The Beehive, 52
Speen, Old Plow, 147

Flowers Draught

Gerrards Cross, The Bull, 113

Flowers I.P.A.

Burford, The Lamb, 20

Kingham, Langston Arms, 37

Flowers Keg

Amersham, The Griffin, 74
Buckingham, White Hart, 91
Goring-on-Thames, Olde Leathern
   Bottel, 32
Linslade, The Globe, 127, 128
Marston Ferry, Victoria Arms, 38

Marsworth, White Lion, 138, 139
Russell's Water, The Beehive, 52
Speen, Old Plow, 147
Tetsworth, The Swan, 59
Wheeler End, Brickmaker's Arms,
   157

Fremlin's Bitter

Cadmore End, Blue Flag, 93

Garne's Special

Burford, The Lamb, 20

Guinness, Draught

Aston Clinton, The Oak, 76
Aylesbury, The Bull's Head, 77, 78
Brill, Sun Hotel, 90
Cadmore End, Blue Flag, 93
Chinnor, The Crown, 22
Colnbrook, The Ostrich, 102
Crowell, Catherine Wheel, 26
Dunsmore, The Fox, 108
Ford, Dinton Hermit, 109
George Green, Double Century, 112
Gibraltar, Bottle and Glass, 114
Great Missenden, The George, 115
  Nag's Head, 116
High Wycombe, White Lion, 121
  Ye Exchange, 122
Linslade, The Globe, 127, 128
Little Missenden, Royal Oak, 130

Little Woolstone, The Barge, 131
Long Crendon, Churchill Arms,
  132
Marsh Gibbon, The Plough, 137
Marston Ferry, Victoria Arms, 38
Pishill, The Crown, 51
Quainton, The Sportsman, 145
Russell's Water, The Beehive, 52
Sandford-on-Thames, King's Arms,
  53
Stony Stratford, The Plough, 149
Swan Bottom, The Gate, 150
Tetsworth, The Swan, 59
Thame, Black Horse, 62
Waddesdon, Crooked Billet, 152,
  153
Whitchurch, White Swan, 158

Hunt Edmunds' Best Bitter

Kingham, Langston Arms, 37

Woodstock, The Bear, 67, 68

Hunt Edmunds' Gold Top

Woodstock, The Bear, 67, 68

Ind Coope Bitter and Mild

Aston Clinton, The Oak, 76
Brill, The Sun, 90
Chinnor, The Crown, 22
  Sir Charles Napier, 22
Crowell, Catherine Wheel, 26
Dunsmore, The Fox, 108
Ford, Dinton Hermit, 109
Gibraltar, Bottle and Glass, 114
Great Missenden, The George, 115
  Nag's Head, 116

High Wycombe, White Lion, 121
  Ye Exchange, 122
Little Missenden, Royal Oak, 130
Long Crendon, Churchill Arms, 132
Oxford, Golden Cross, 44
Quainton, The Sportsman, 145
Thame, Black Horse, 62
Waddesdon, Crooked Billet, 152,
  153
Whitchurch, White Swan, 158

Light Ale, Draught
Eynsham, Red Lion, 30

Mann's Bitter
Lane End, Clayton Arms, 125

Mann's I.P.A. and Mild
High Wycombe, The Falcon, 120

Mead, Cornish
Milton Common, Three Pigeons, 39

Mitchell & Butler's Brew II
Banbury, The Inn Within, 13   Tetsworth, The Swan, 59
Oxford, Turl Tavern, 49

Mitchell & Butler's Mild
Kingham, Langston Arms, 37   Oxford, Turl Tavern, 49

Morland's Bitter
Dorchester-on-Thames, The   Pishill, The Crown, 51
    George, 28

'Noggin' Keg
Adstock, Folly Inn, 73   Stony Stratford, The Plough, 149

'Owd Roger' Beer
Forty Green, Royal Standard of
    England, 110

Port and Sherry from the Barrel
High Wycombe, The Falcon, 120

Simonds Draught Beer
Wexham, Red Lion, 156

Tavern Keg
George Green, Double Century, 112   Hedgerley, The One Pin, 119

Varsity Keg Bitter
Eynsham, Red Lion, 30   Marsh Gibbon, The Plough, 137

Tolly Draught
Gerrards Cross, The Bull, 113   Linslade, The Globe, 127, 128

Watney's Bitter
Linslade, The Globe, 127, 128

Watney's Red Barrel
Aston Clinton, The Oak, 76
Bledlow, Red Lions, 84
Brill, Sun Hotel, 90
Chesham, White Horse, 101
Chinnor, Sir Charles Napier, 22
Crowell, Catherine Wheel, 26
Dunsmore, The Fox, 108
Ford, Dinton Hermit, 109
Gibraltar, Bottle and Glass, 114
Great Missenden, The George, 115
    Nag's Head, 116
High Wycombe, The Falcon, 120
    Ye Exchange, 122
Linslade, The Globe, 127, 128
Little Missenden, Royal Oak, 130

Long Crendon, Churchill Arms, 132
Minster Lovell, Old Swan, 40
Pishill, The Crown, 51
Princes Risborough, The Pink and
    Lily, 143
Quainton, The Sportsman, 145
Russell's Water, The Beehive, 52
Tetsworth, The Swan, 59
Thame, Black Horse, 62
Waddesdon, Crooked Billet, 152,
    153
Wendover, King and Queen, 154
Wheeler End, Brickmaker's Arms,
    157
Whitchurch, White Swan, 158

Whitbread
Banbury, The Inn Within, 13
Buckingham, White Hart, 91

Marston Ferry, Victoria Arms, 38
Wexham, Red Lion, 156

174

Whitbread Tankard

Benson-on-Thames, Chicken in the Basket, 16, 17
Bix, The Fox, 19
Cadmore End, Blue Flag, 93
Dorchester-on-Thames, The George, 28
Goring-on-Thames, Olde Leatherne Bottel, 32
Henley-on-Thames, The Angel, 33, 34
Kingham, Langston Arms, 37
Marsworth, White Lion, 138, 139
Oxford, Turl Tavern, 49
Penn, The Crown, 141, 142
Pishill, The Crown, 51
Princes Risborough, Three Horse-shoes, 144

Wines

High Wycombe, The Falcon, 120
Marlow, Hare and Hounds, 134

Worthington 'E'

Amersham, The Griffin, 74
Aylesbury, The King's Head, 81
Banbury, The Inn Within, 13
Bledlow, Red Lions, 84
Buckingham, White Hart, 91
Burford, The Lamb, 20
Forty Green, Royal Standard of England, 110
Kingham, Langston Arms, 37
Linslade, The Globe, 127
Oxford, Turl Tavern, 49
Princes Risborough, Three Horse-shoes, 144
Russell's Water, The Beehive, 52
Speen, Old Plow, 147
Swan Bottom, The Gate, 150
Tetsworth, The Swan, 59
Wheeler End, Brickmaker's Arms, 157
Woodstock, The Bear, 67

Younger's Bitter

Adstock, Folly Inn, 73
Marston Ferry, Victoria Arms, 38
Marsworth, White Lion, 138, 139
Princes Risborough, Three Horse-shoes, 144
Wheeler End, Brickmaker's Arms, 157
Winslow, The Bell, 159

Younger's Scotch Ale

Marston Ferry, Victoria Arms, 38
Oxford, Turl Tavern, 49
Swan Bottom, The Gate, 150

Younger's 'Tartan'

Cadmore End, Blue Flag, 93